Letters of Love

Mariia Biriukova

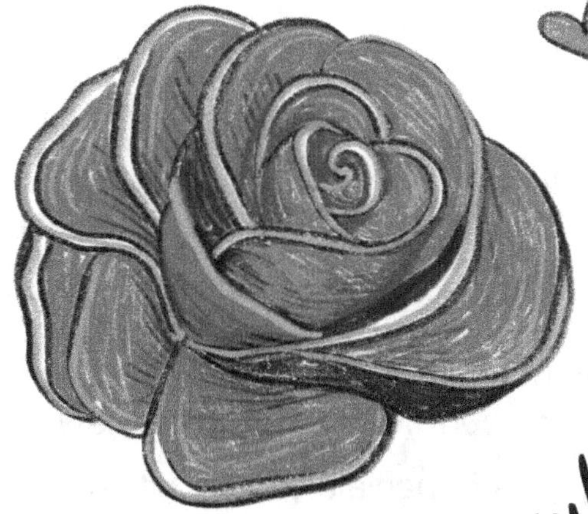

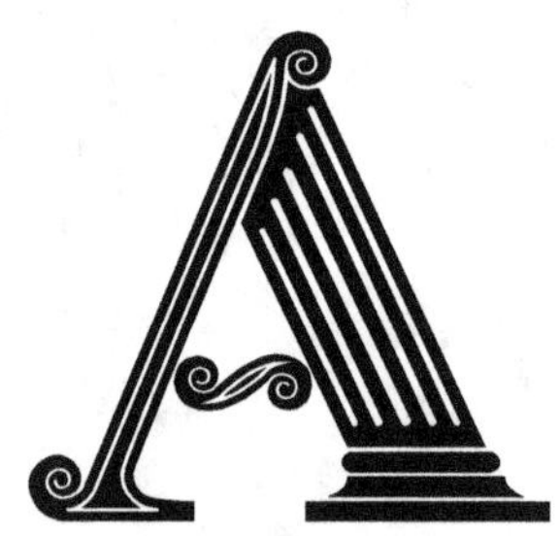

Letters of Love

A Heartfelt Journey Through Hand-Lettering, Coloring, and Meaningful Reflections
© 2024 by Special Art

For permissions, contact: support@specialartbooks.com

Published by Special Art Books | www.specialartbooks.com

Paperback ISBN: 9791255531944

Images © Shutterstock

This book
belongs to

. . . .

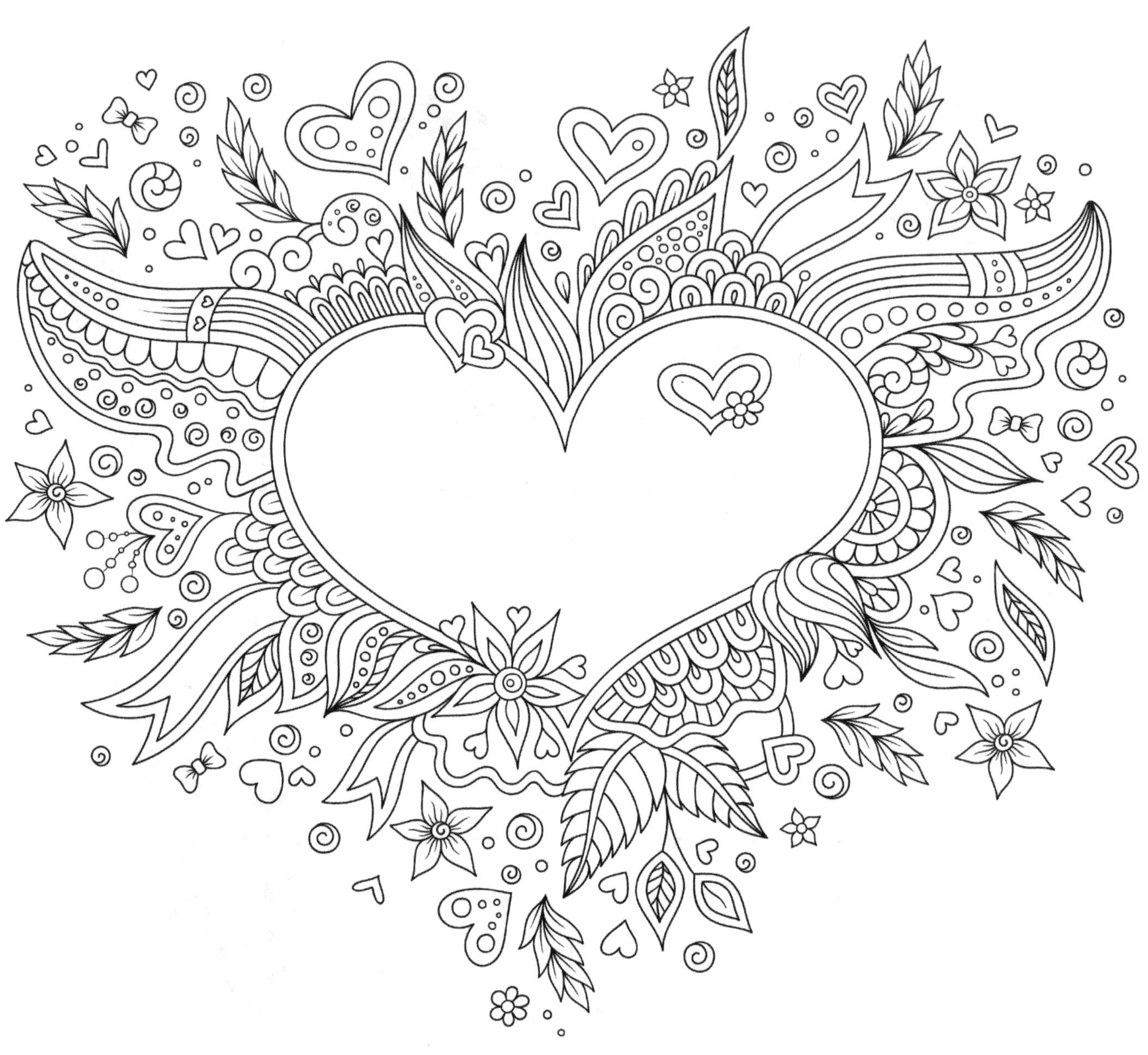

TABLE OF CONTENTS

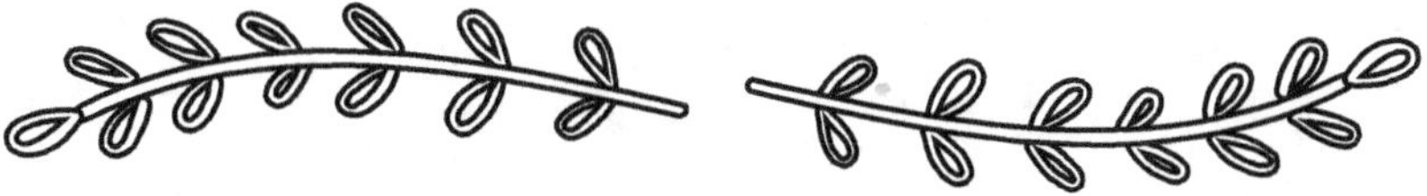

INTRODUCTION

You are worthy of love and compassion. And you are capable of showing love and compassion to others. Inside these pages, you'll discover how you can creatively express your emotions. *Welcome to Letters of Love*!

In this book, you'll journey through the different expressions of love. You'll learn to embrace self-acceptance while using your lettering and coloring skills. You'll learn how to show self-care through creative projects and explore a range of lettering styles, warm colors, and inspiring quotes that celebrate love in all its forms.

Throughout *Letters of Love*, you'll color in illustrations that speak of love, care, and understanding, encouraging you to love yourself and nurture your relationships with others. As you progress, you'll build on old and new techniques to enrich your creative journey and personal growth.

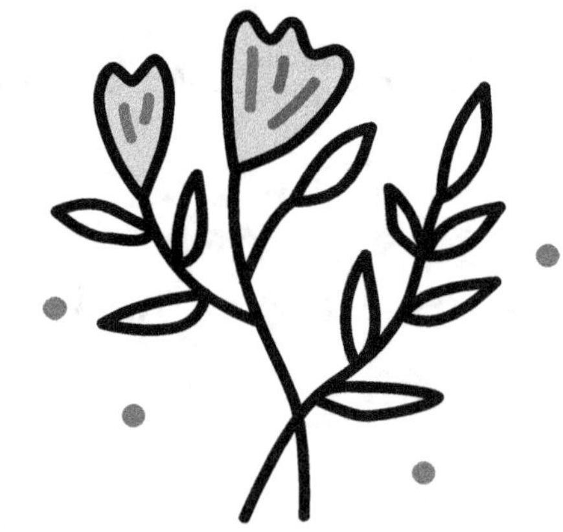

This book has a distinctive monochrome design for a reason. You will be the one to color each page, and with each reflection and expression of your emotions of love, this book will bloom into a colorful journal that you can cherish.

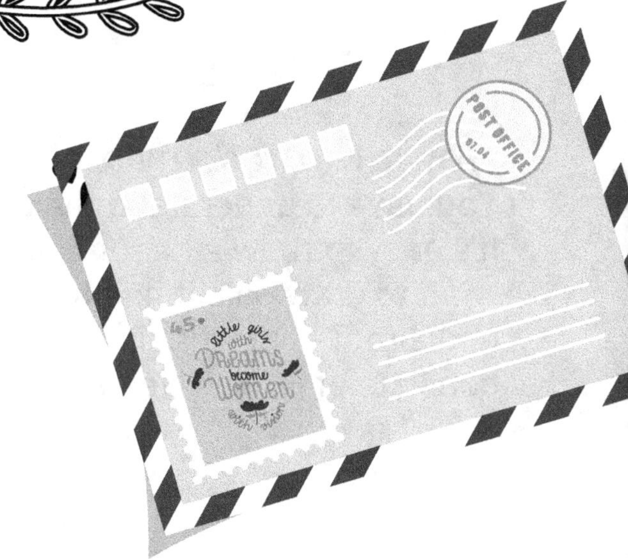

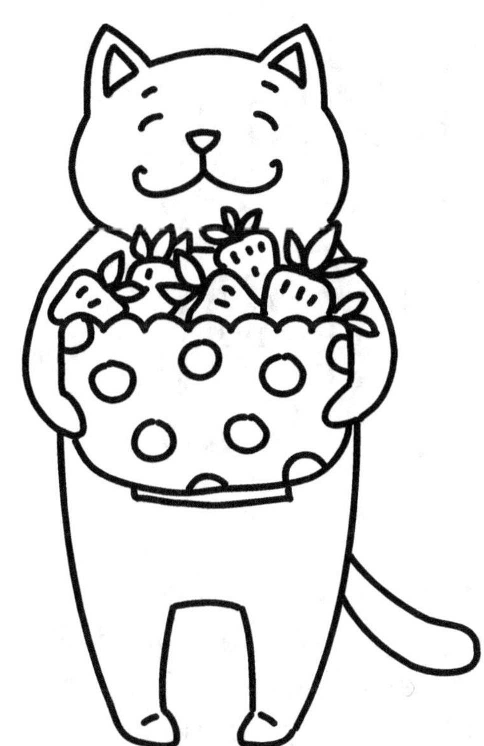

How you use this book is entirely up to you. You can use whatever colors you feel expresses your thoughts and reflections most. Write on it, color it, scribble your notes and reflections on it. Remember, there's no formula for love. Let your sentiments flow, genuine and true, painting a unique tale of love that's all about you.

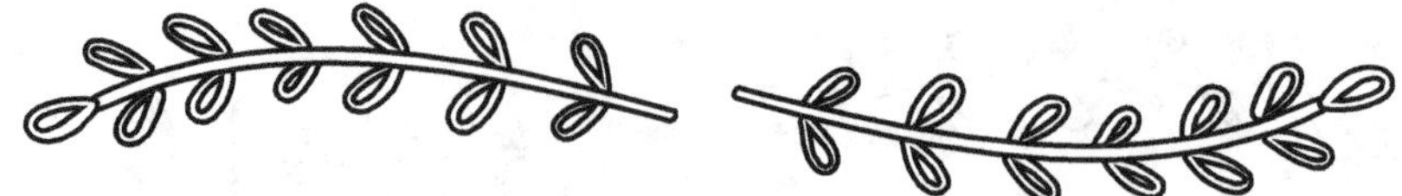

How do you draw an emotion?
You have to understand the elements that make up the scene.
It's easy to draw a cat or a house, for example, because we know exactly what to draw - a cat has four paws and a tail, a house has walls, windows and a roof - but what is love? In this book, we will gradually define what it consists of. We will learn how to notice it and how to cultivate it.

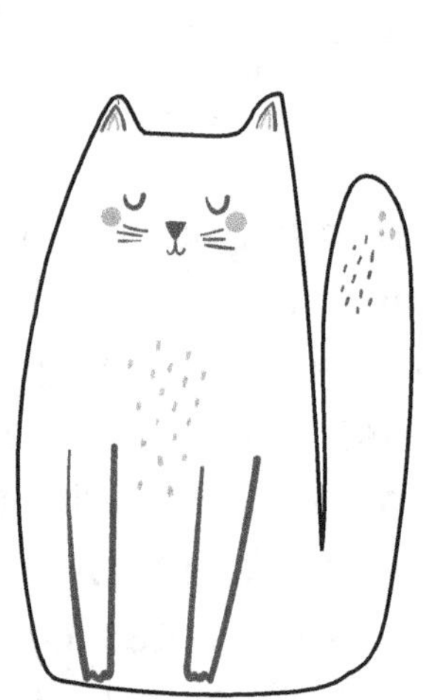

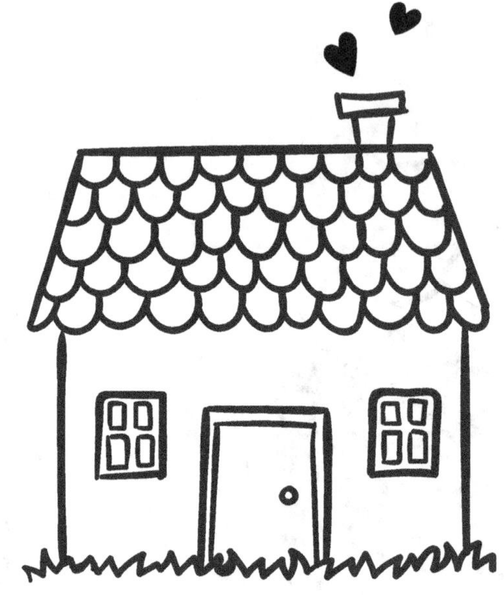

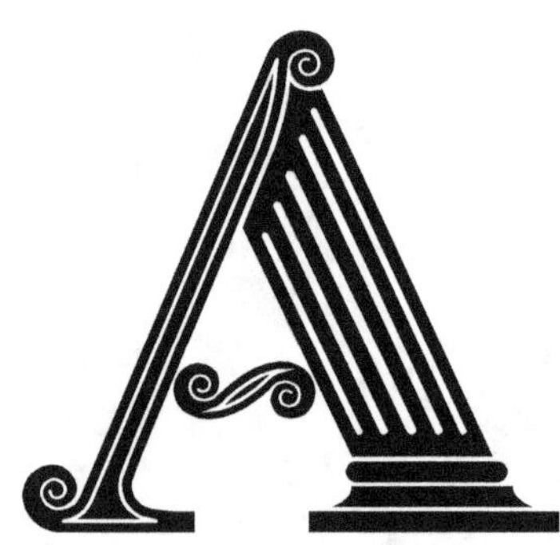

Art makes an impression on a person.
Art has an effect that can help people evolve, develop spiritually and find balance and harmony. Since ancient times, art has been used as therapy for the soul.
And here we are talking about who creates a piece of art and who has the opportunity to see a masterpiece.

In this book, we will create love, using calligraphy and coloring. Getting started with calligraphy is actually not as hard as it seems.

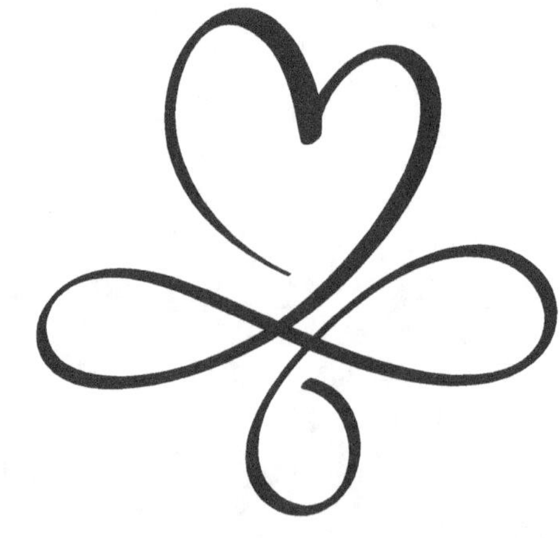

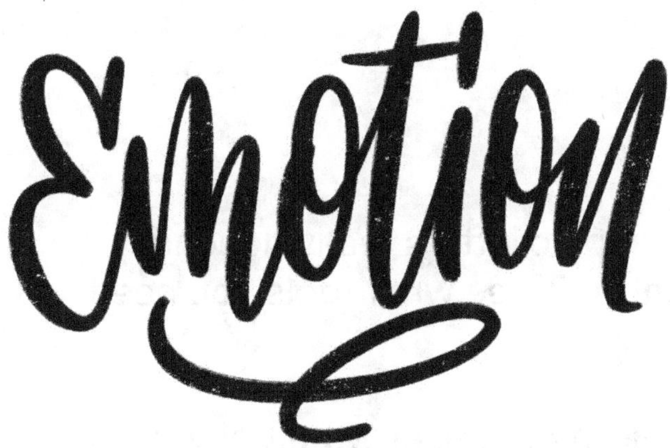

Calligraphy is the art of beautiful writing. The shape of the letters is completely dependent on the writing tool and the movement of the hand.

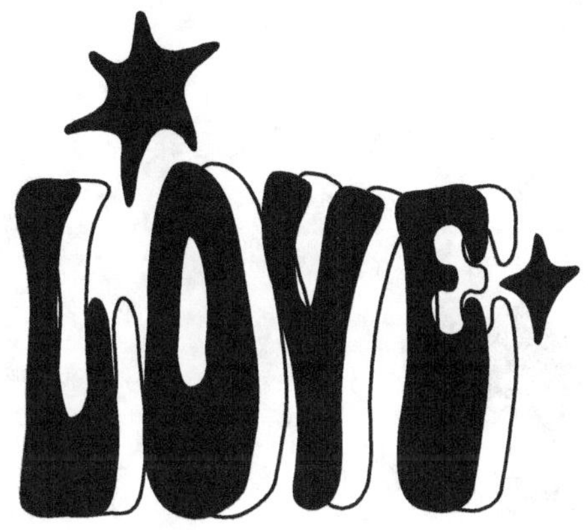

Lettering is the art of drawing letters. Letters are created uniquely for a particular lettering. This means that the shape, style, and other stylistic elements should be subordinate to the main idea and meaning of the phrase.

But both calligraphy and lettering have the task of creating unique pieces of art that create the atmosphere and mood of a phrase before you read the letters.

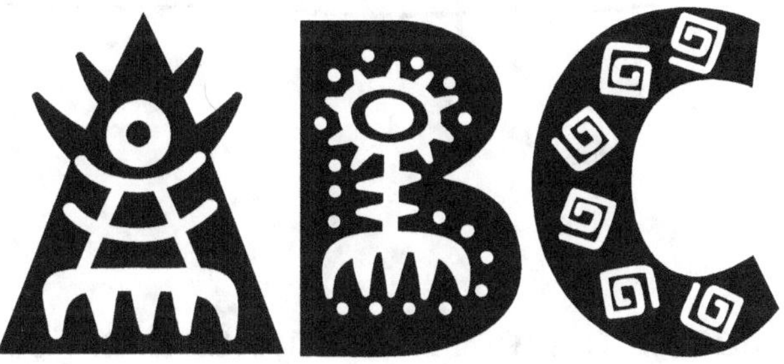

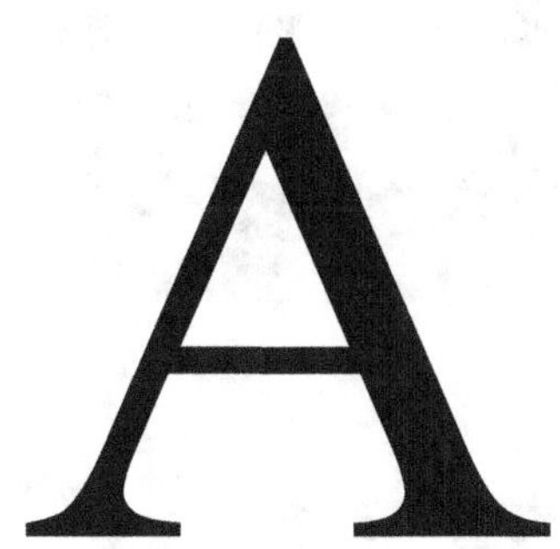

Actually - any typeface has a shape and creates a certain look - but the fonts that are used for large blocks of text are designed to make the reading experience as comfortable as possible. If you're reading a book and you're not paying attention to the typeface, it's a good type. But the opposite is true of display fonts - a neutral sign on the street will not catch the eye or attract customers.

The shape of the letters should always match the task and the meaning.

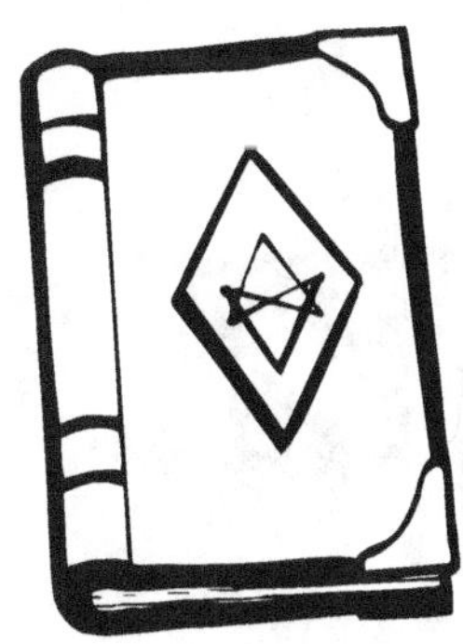

Since the shape of calligraphic letters really depends on the writing instrument, let's see what tools you need in this book.

You can color with pencils, markers, or watercolors; there is a big space for options. Watercolor Brush Pens would be a great choice.

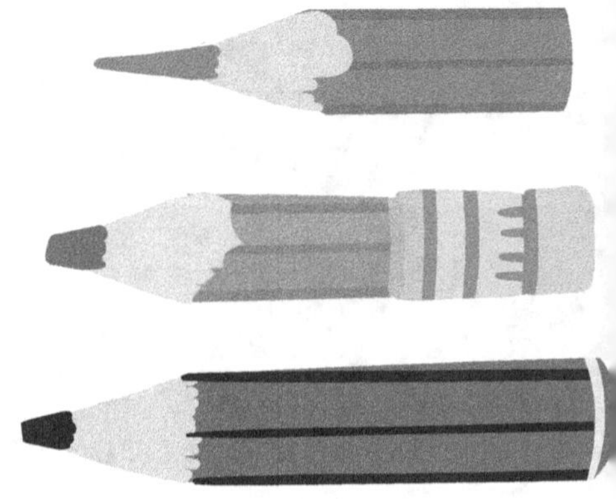

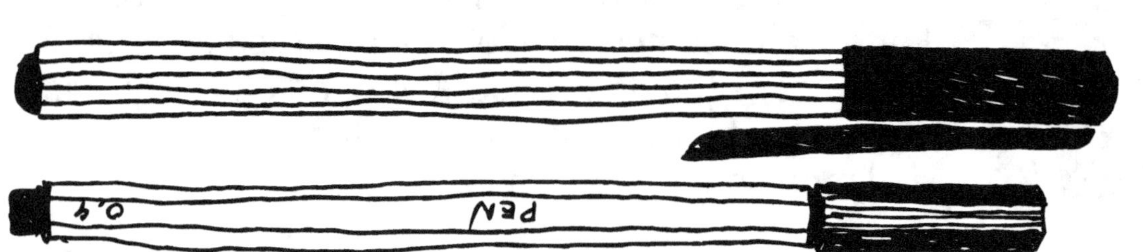

Classic calligraphy is nib and ink, but writing with a nib requires absorbent paper and space to dip the nib in the ink. So it will be easier to use modern tools, special calligraphy markers: Pentel Brush Sign Pen, Tombow Fudenosuke, Ecoline Brush Pen, Sharpie Brush Marker.

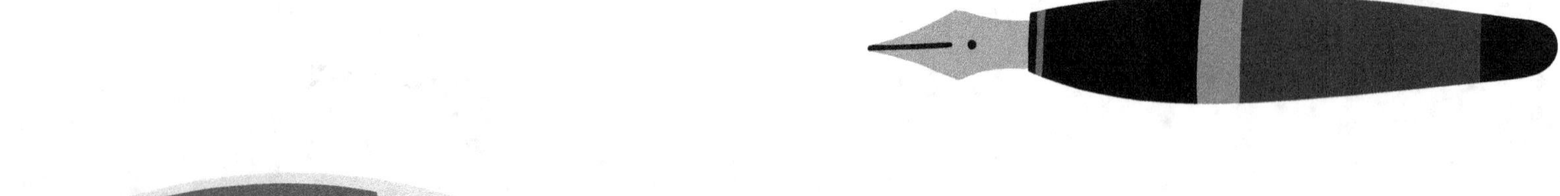

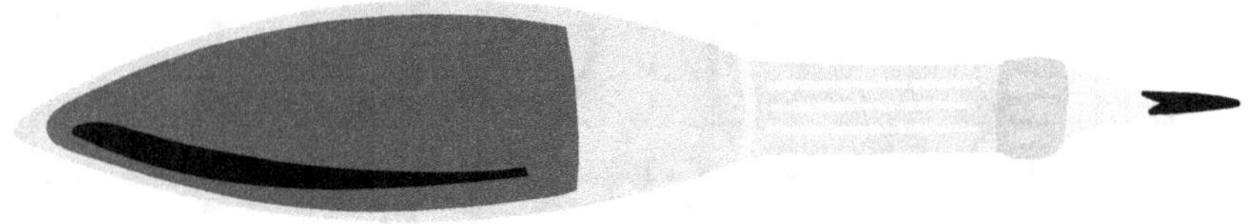

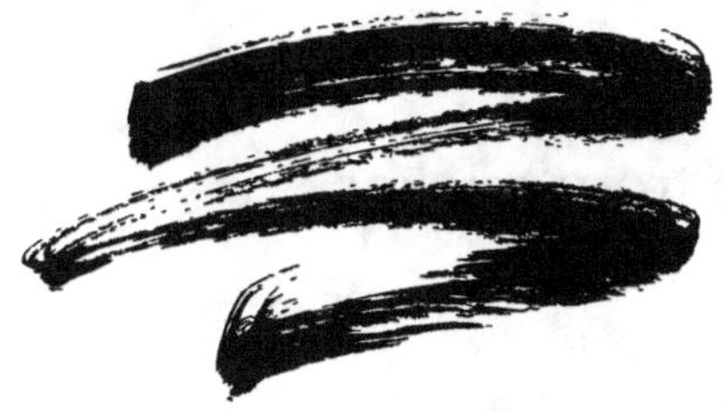

When using various coloring tools such as colored pencils, markers, or watercolors, it's essential to be mindful of potential color bleeding. To protect your artwork and maintain vibrant results, we recommend placing a save sheet or scrap paper between the pages while coloring. This practice helps prevent colors from transferring to adjacent pages and ensures a cleaner finished product.

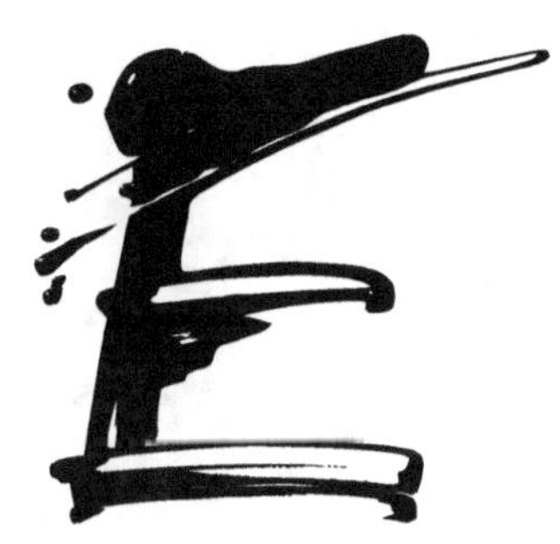

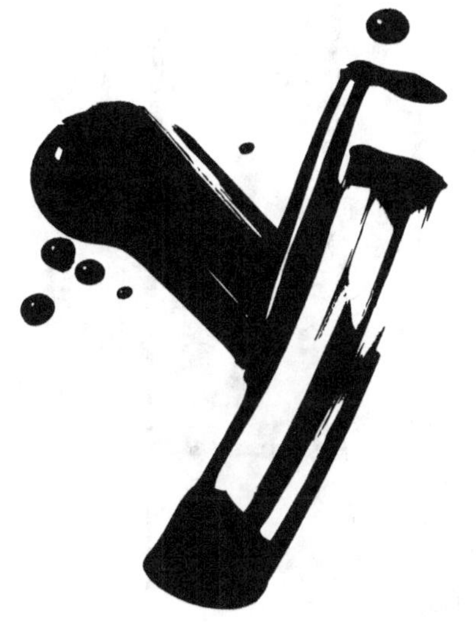

Embracing imperfections is an integral part of the creative journey. Throughout the book, remember that perceived imperfections, like color smudges or bleeding, contribute to unique and beautiful results. View these moments as opportunities for growth and self-expression.

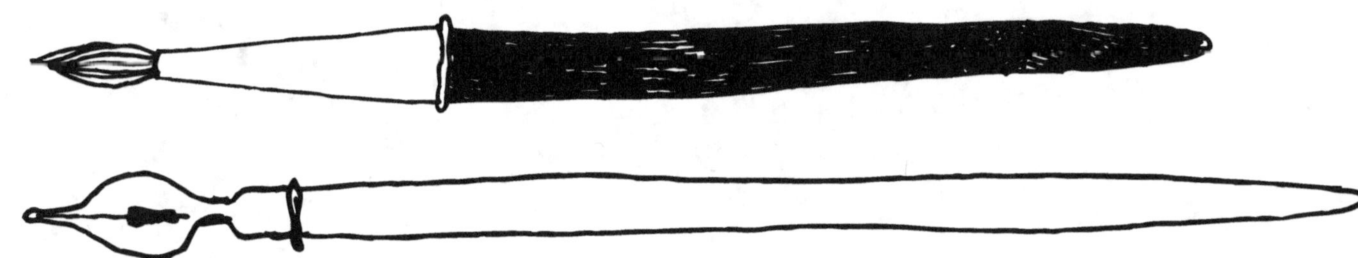

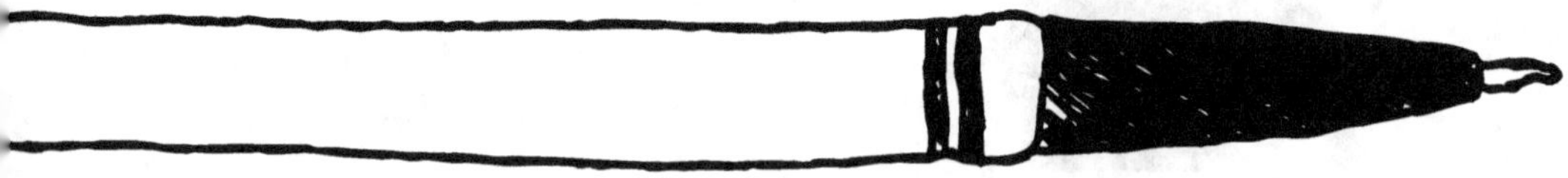

To enhance your coloring experience, consider using a removable and foldable coloring workspace made from thicker paper or cardboard. This workspace can be attached to the book spine or included in an envelope on the back cover. Featuring inspirational quotes and motifs related to the book's theme, the visually appealing workspace can serve as an added layer of protection and inspiration while coloring.

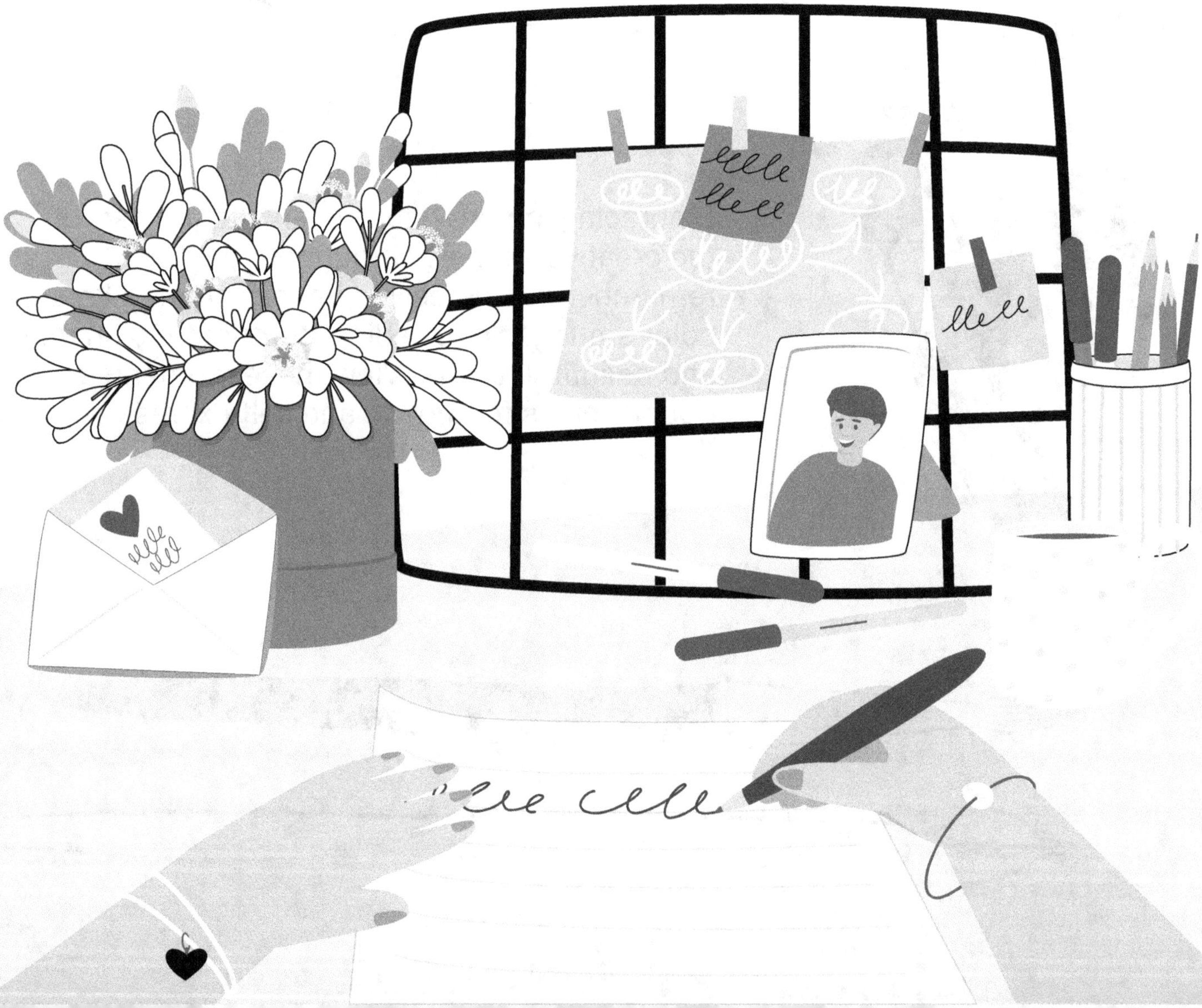

Self-love is an important part of self-care.
When you're ready to reset and recharge,
you can use these tips as inspiration to
love yourself more.

♥ Make time for focused work on the emotion

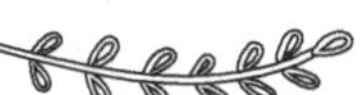

♥ Make sure no one can distract you, so that you're
not bothered by outside noises

♥ Turn time with this book into a date with yourself

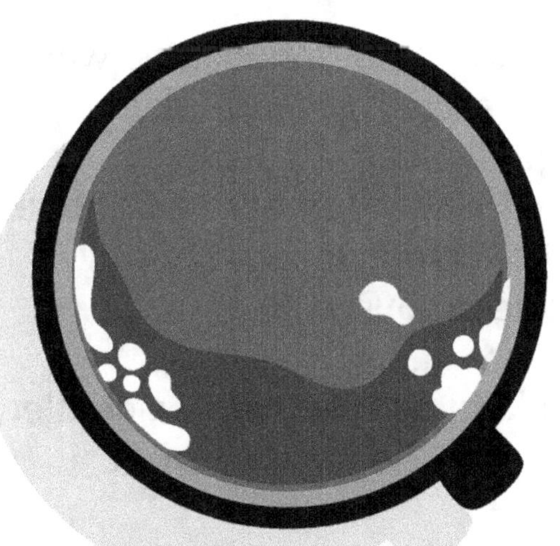

♥ Take care of yourself by choosing a comfortable
and beautiful spot and thinking about things that
make you feel good - a nice cup of tea, a cold
drink, or something else.

♥ Create the right atmosphere - surround yourself
with objects you associate with love, remind you
of the people you love, put on romantic music, set
the lights, perhaps light some candles.

So, are you ready to embark on this new adventure
and explore the world of love and self-compassion
through the art of lettering and coloring? Let's
begin our journey together, and witness the
transformative power of love in your life and
creative pursuits. Welcome to *Letters of Love.* ♥

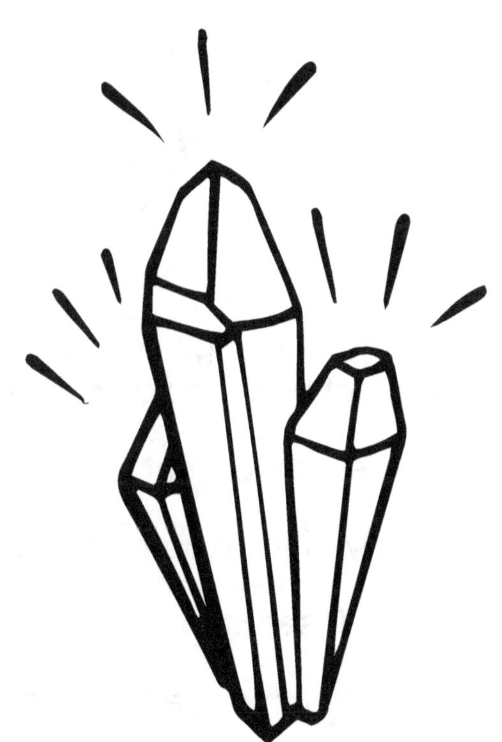

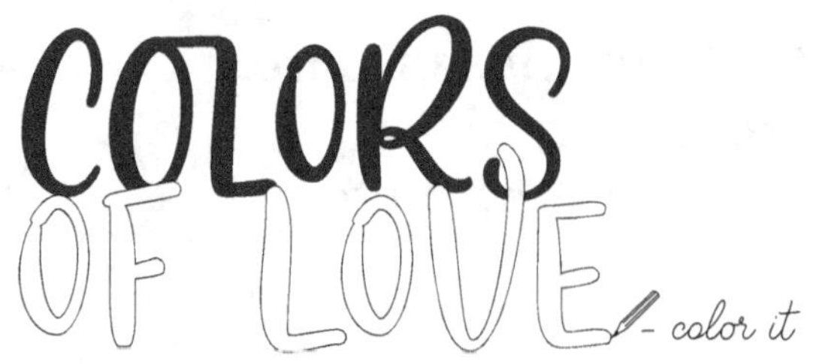

Color is an important element in any kind of art.
An artist often uses colors to convey his or her emotions
through the paintings of visual artistry. So for a better output,
some color exercises for artists are helpful.

Find a pleasant experience of a happy relationship in your memory. What colors might you associate that memory with? Capture the color palette you saw in that memory and use it to tune into those emotions of love and happy relationships.

♥ *Red* is a warm color associated with passion, love, energy, anger, and excitement. It's easy to see why - blood is red, and when our hearts beat and emotions soar, this red hue is often visible on our skin.

♥ If we're talking about a calmer, gentler manifestation - we can use *pink*.

♥ *Purple* is also associated with softness, caress, and blooming flowers.

Color meanings don't exist in a vacuum; there are lots of factors that impact how we perceive them. Some of these factors include:

♥ Their shade, tint or tone

♥ How they're combined with other colors

♥ Their saturation

♥ How they're paired with other design elements like fonts and shapes.

color it

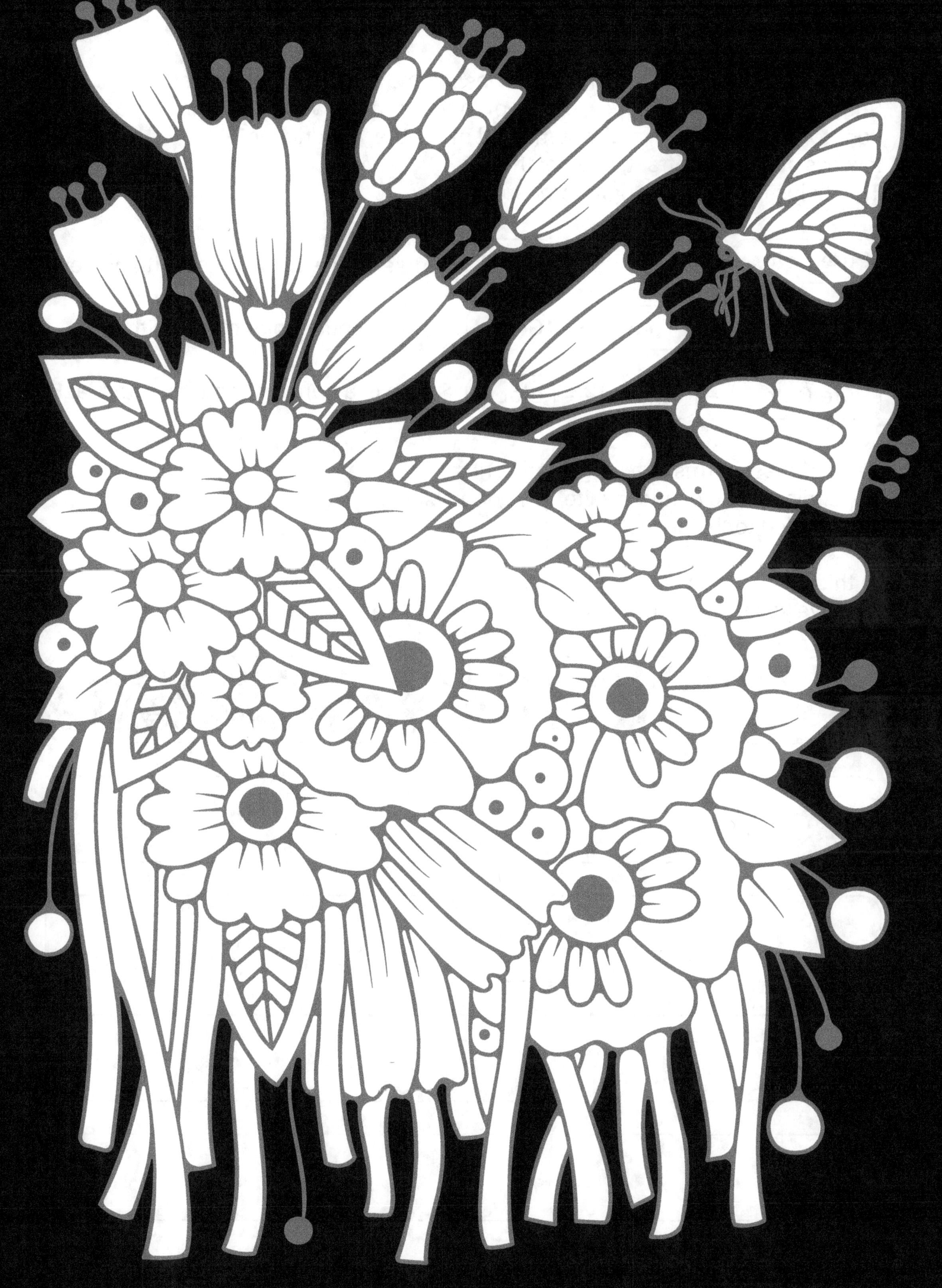

Why is it so important?
Using only pure colors simplifies the design and makes it look flatter.
Shades, shadows, and tones, on the other hand, allow you to create
light-tonal perspective, and volume and make the work richer
in ways such as contrast, and depth.
This helps to create the right atmosphere.

| Pure Color | → | Tint | ← | White | Tint is a pure color mixed with white.

| Pure Color | → | Tone | ← | Gray | Tone is a pure color mixed with gray.

| Pure Color | → | Shade | ← | Black | Shade is a pure color mixed with black.

Each of these terms is a range and varies
depending on how much white, gray, or black you
have added to the pure color.

In this way, knowing how to blend color correctly
will give you unlimited possibilities.

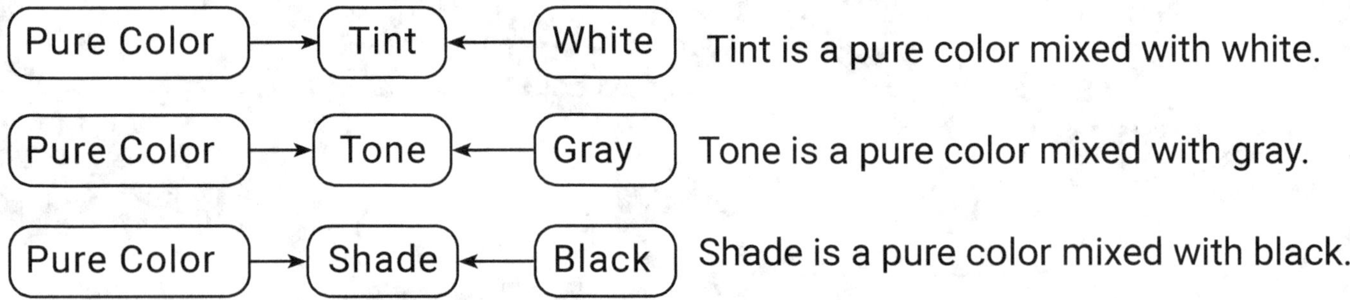

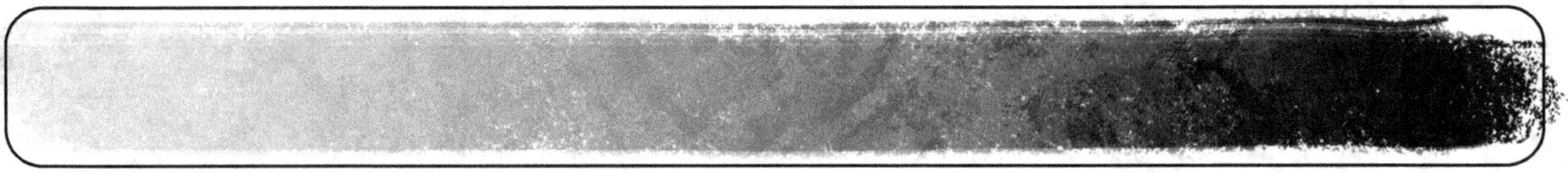

Let's try to make a smooth transition from white to black in 7 steps.

white ·································· ►*black*

Where 1 is pure white and 7 is deep black.
Remember that black is a strong color and add it gradually,
controlling the level of darkening.

Now make the transition in 4 steps.

The aim is to learn to do the
dimming in the same step. See
visually how much darkening you
need to do to get the shade you
want.

Repeat the same exercise with other colors - creating a gradient from
pure color to black, white or gray.

Doing color swatches is a great exercise. It helps to become
sufficiently familiar with the materials - how does this marker
behave on this paper - what if you add water?
What if you paint in 2-3 layers?

And of course - mixing colors - color A + color B = ?

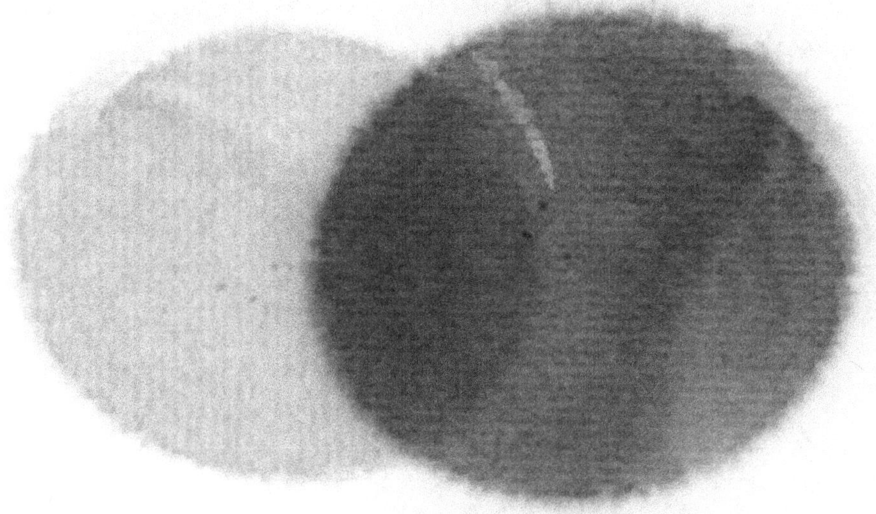

Make color swatches and color combinations in different
materials. Come back to this page as you work through
the book and make variations of the color palette - this
will help you match the colors more harmoniously!

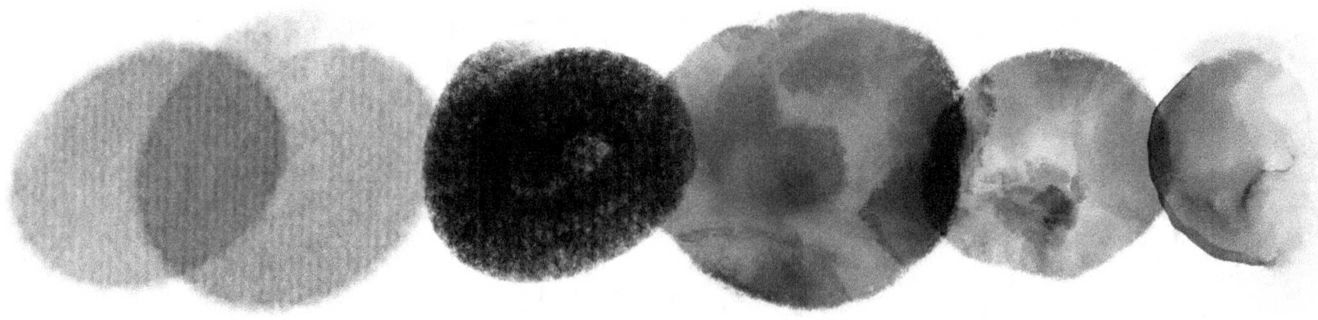

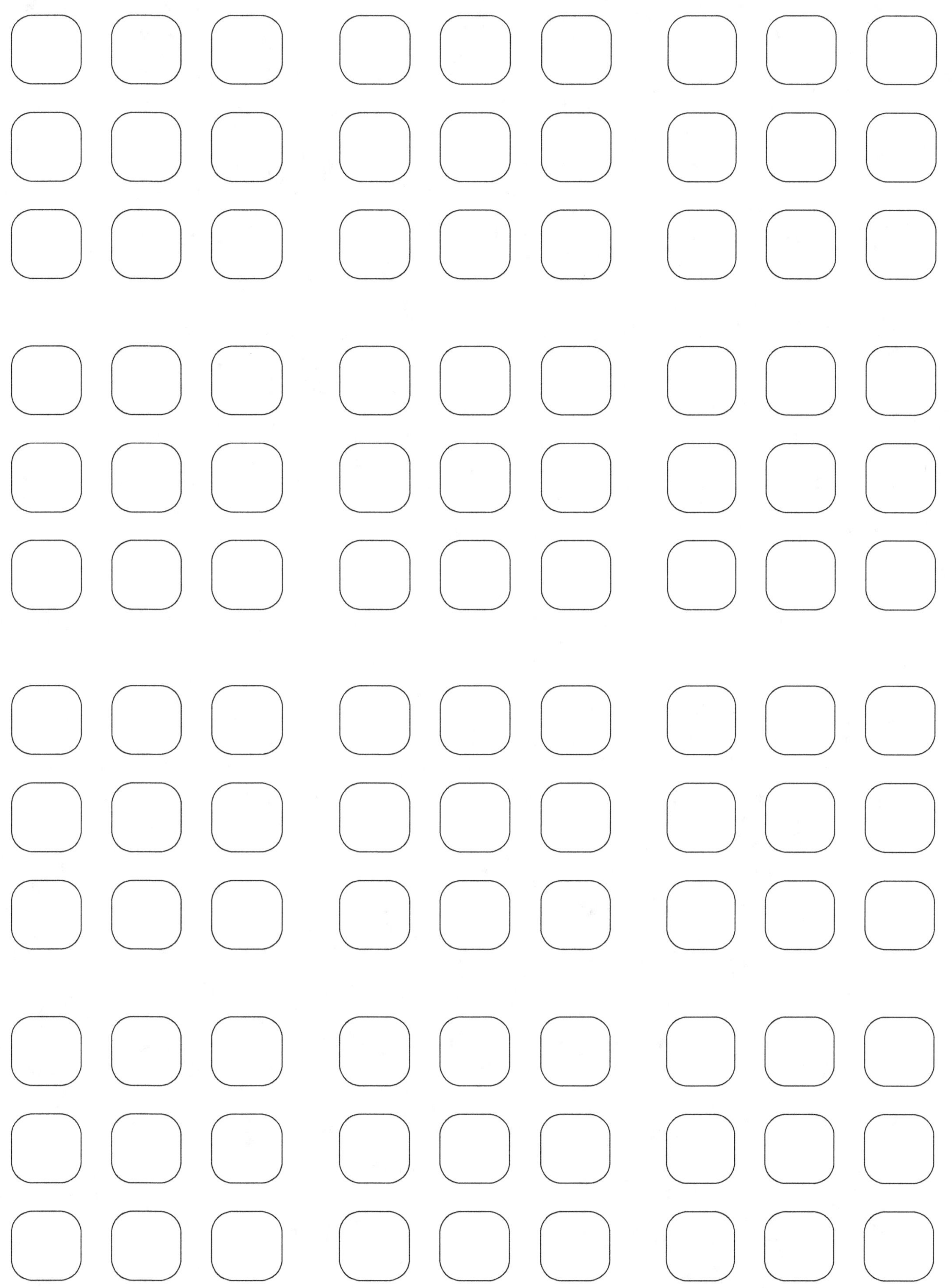

True LOVE stories NEVER have endings

BASICS OF LETTERING

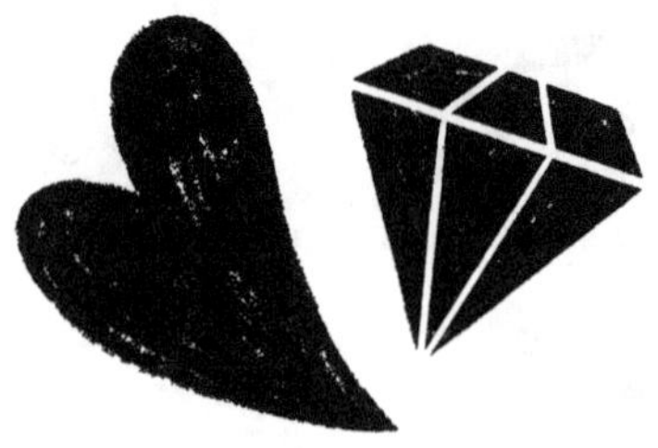

Calligraphy is an art of beautiful writing that requires time, attention and concentration. And what is love? It is when you pay attention, give time and focus on what you love. In this way calligraphy helps us to build this connection and learn the art of love!

First, you need to get familiar with the basic strokes. Every time we write down, we add pressure. So that the line comes out thick. When writing upwards, we draw a thin line without pressure.

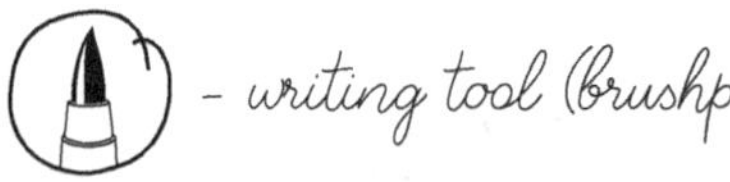 - writing tool (brushpen)

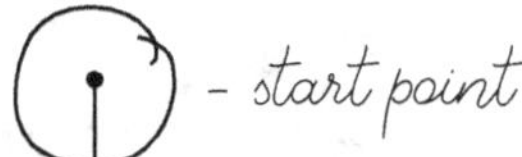 - start point

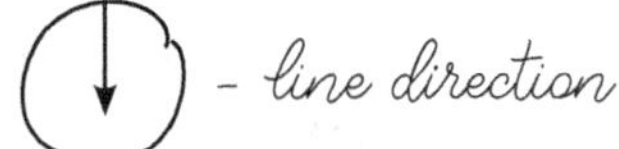 - line direction

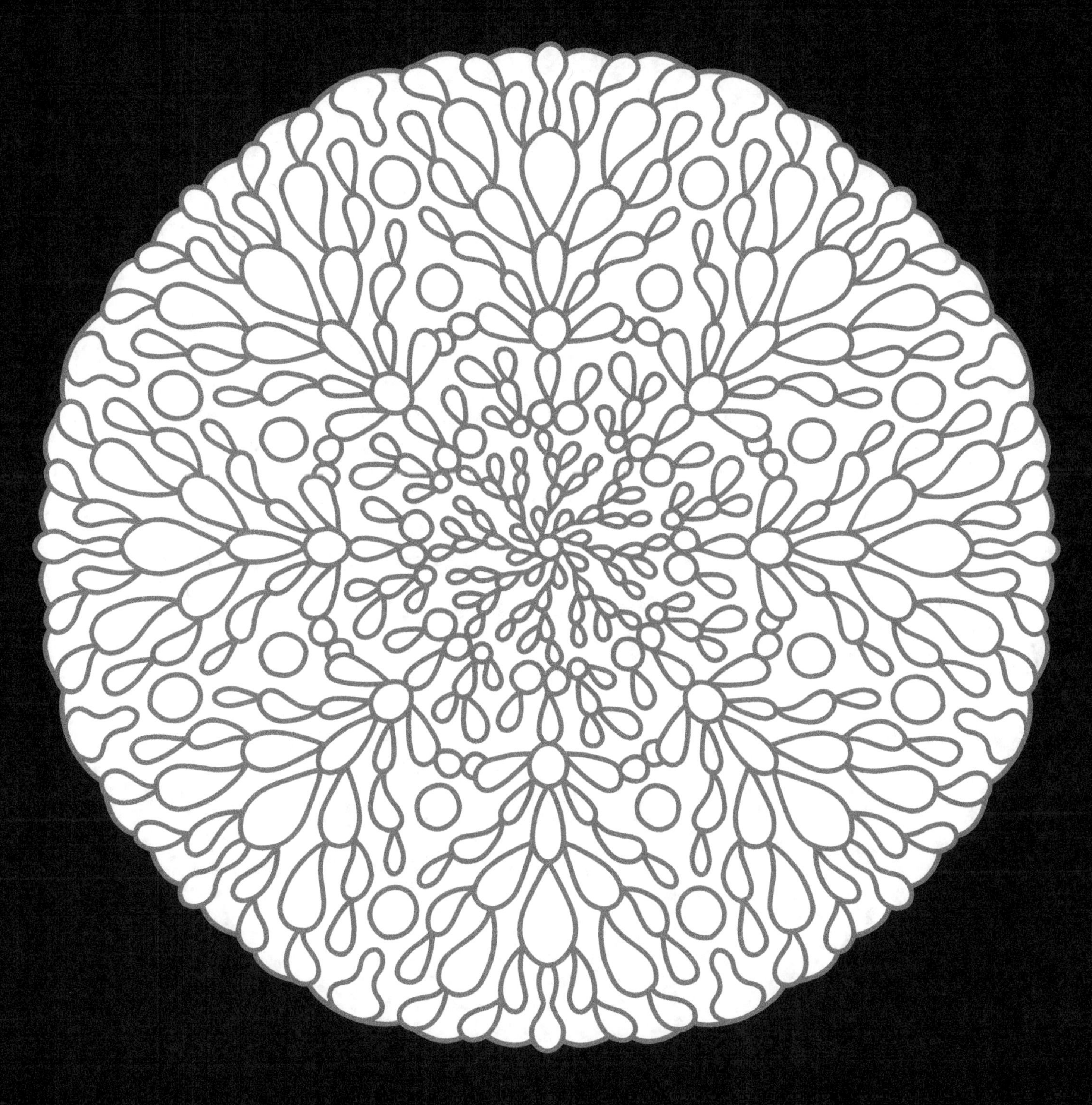

Next, you need to develop a smooth transition. Make sure that the strokes do not merge with each other, and that the flow from thin to thick strokes is smooth, without angles or sharp transitions.

In the world of lettering, every stroke of the pen becomes a dance of emotions, where each curve and loop carries the weight of our feelings. Just as love and self-compassion evolve and grow with time, so do the graceful lines and flowing letters on the page.

Continue to practice these basic strokes on separate pieces of paper. Downstrokes are heavy, like the burden of emotions unspoken. Release this burden on each downstroke. Upstrokes are thin and light—the freedom of emotions expressed and the lightness of being able to show what you truly feel inside.

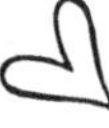

ELEGANT
LETTERING STYLES – color it

As we learn to craft these enchanting letters, we also learn to express the depth of our emotions with finesse and grace. In this chapter, we will practice an airy and delicate script as well as a rapid and incisive script. These are two almost opposite styles, but both express a range of emotions.

For the airy and delicate script, smoothly apply pressure as you move your hand down. Gently release pressure toward the end of the line and smoothly move to the next element. While you practice the strokes, remember the ease of falling in love and the smoothness of a relationship that stands the test of time. Love is delicate but strong; it gives you lightness of feeling and transcends your physical state into a state of calm and elegance.

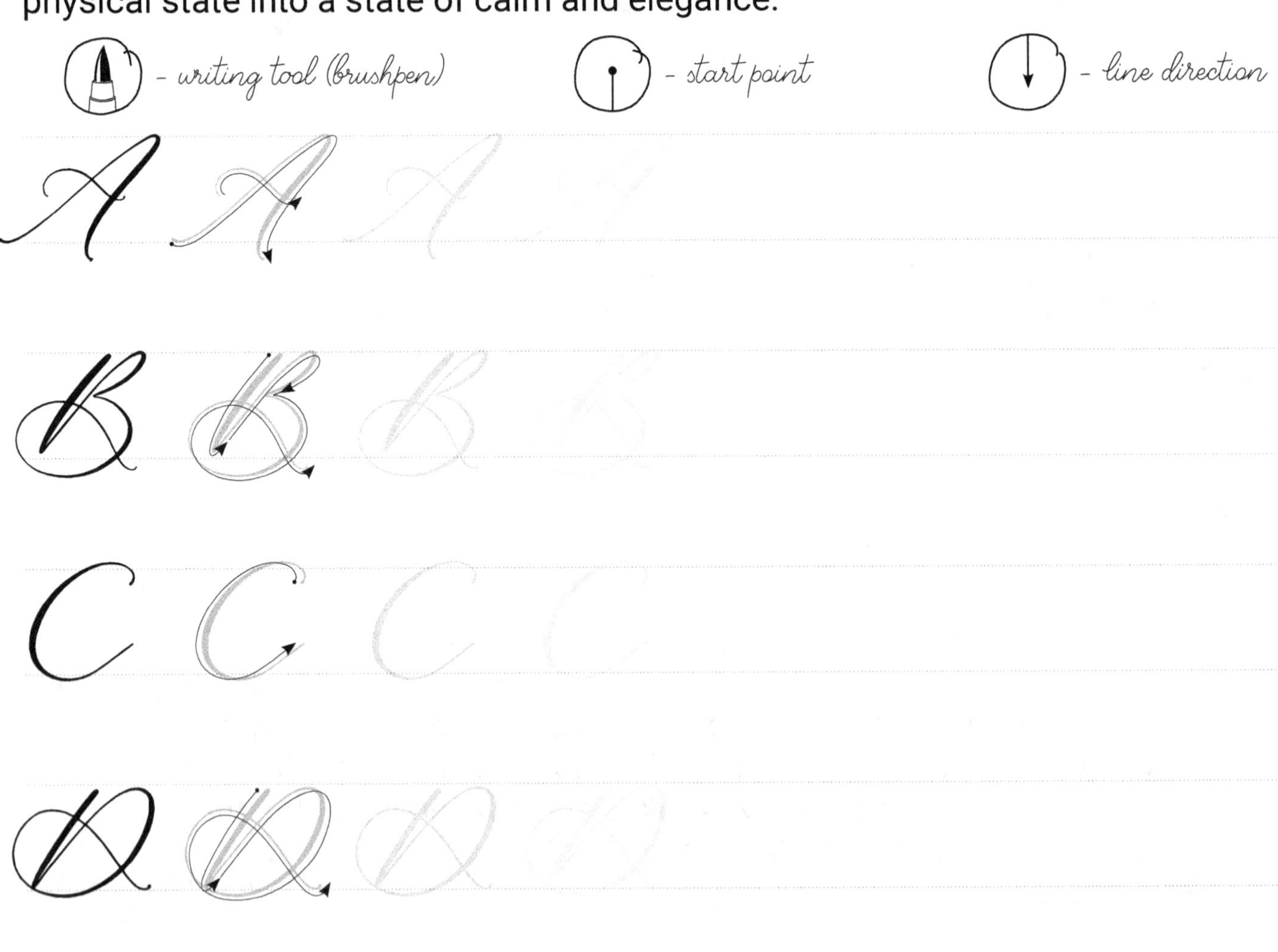

Each stroke becomes an expression of our innermost thoughts, a reflection of the love we hold within, and a testament to the compassion we extend to ourselves. Just as the ink flows effortlessly, our emotions find their way onto the canvas of paper, where they take shape and form, transforming into a tangible representation of our journey towards self-discovery.

♥ Follow the guidelines and use the blank space for practice

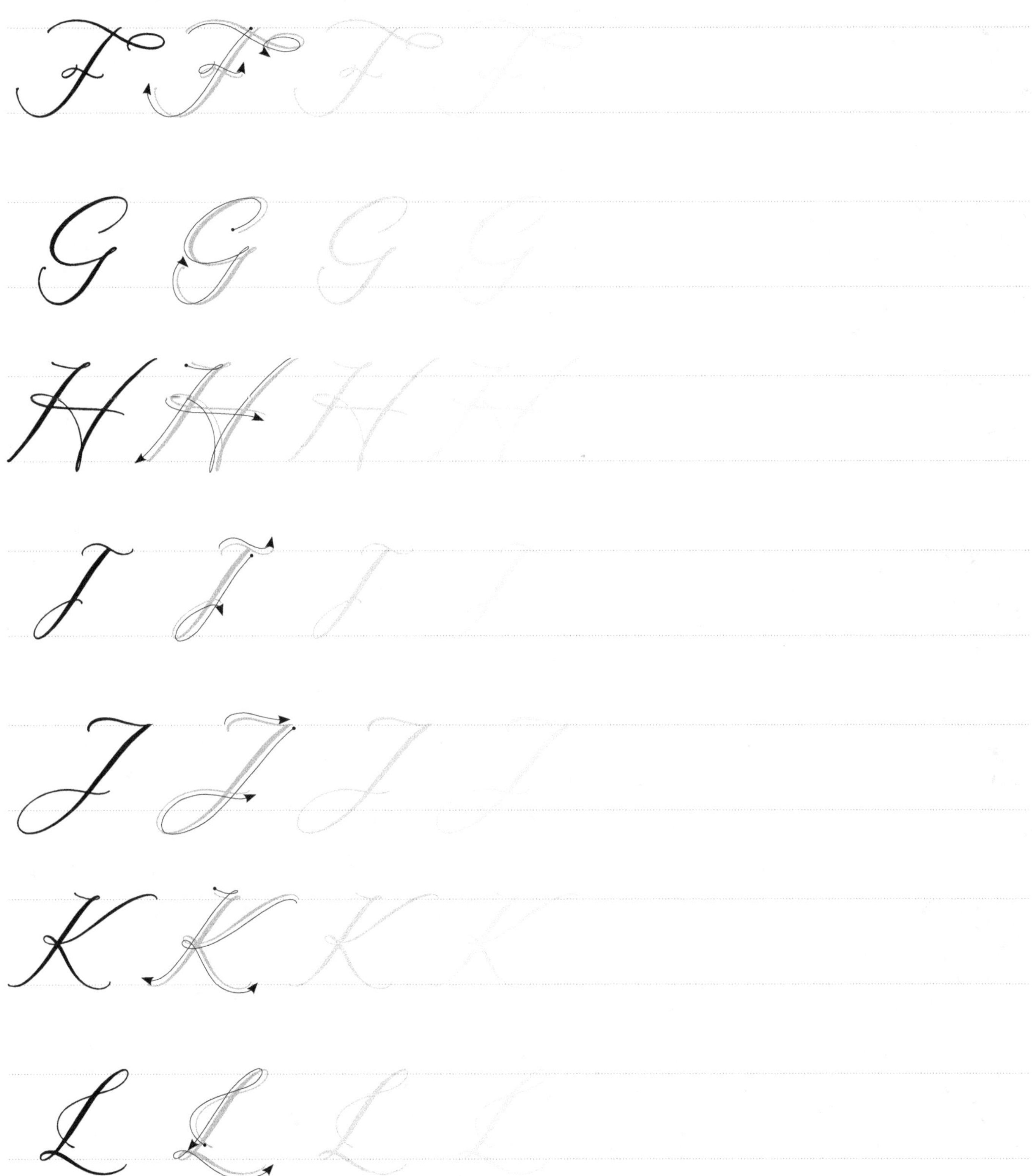

With every letter we form, we find a little piece of ourselves, and in the art of elegant lettering, we learn to embrace the beauty of our emotions and share them with the world around us.

♥ Follow the guidelines and use the blank space for practice

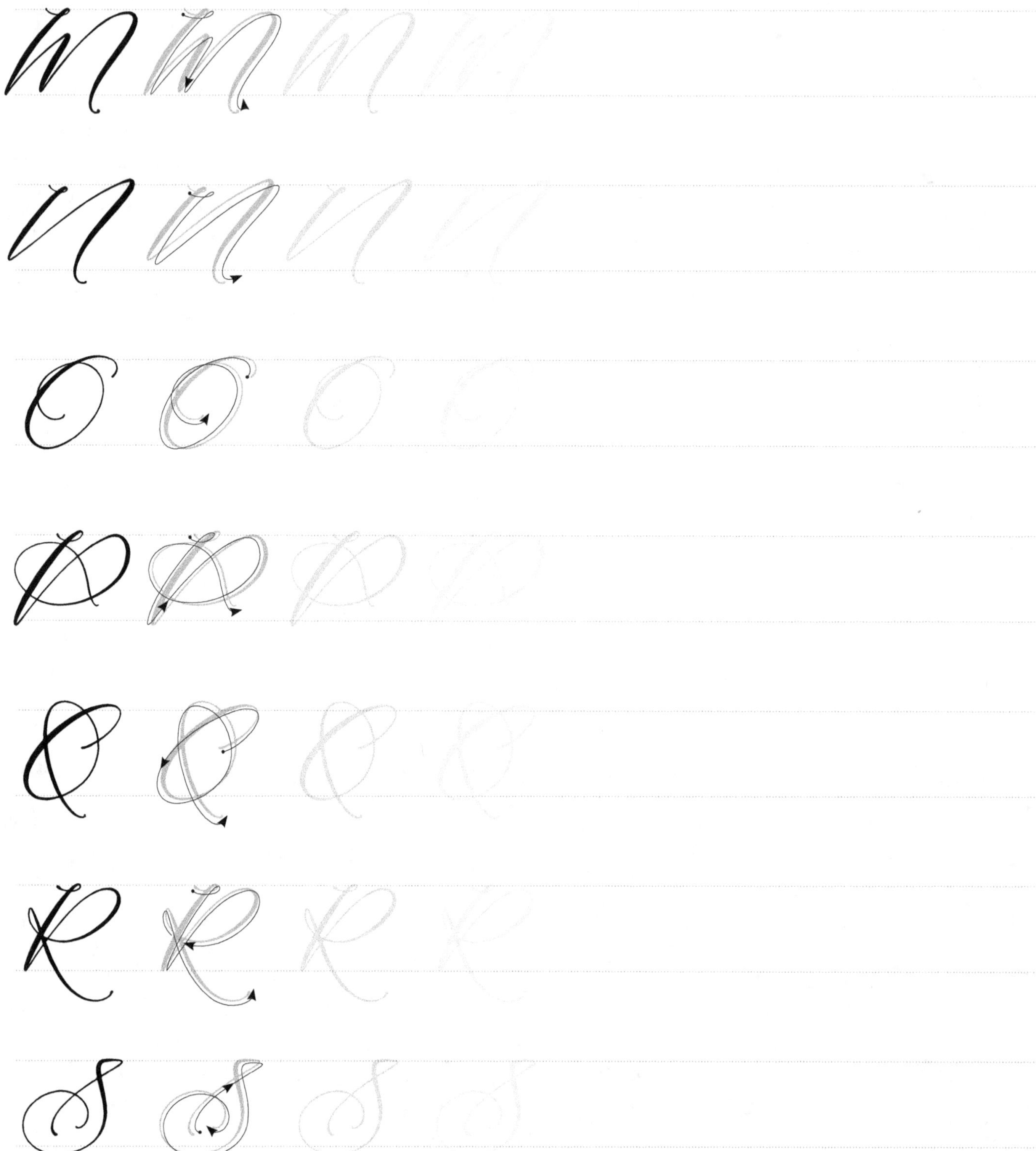

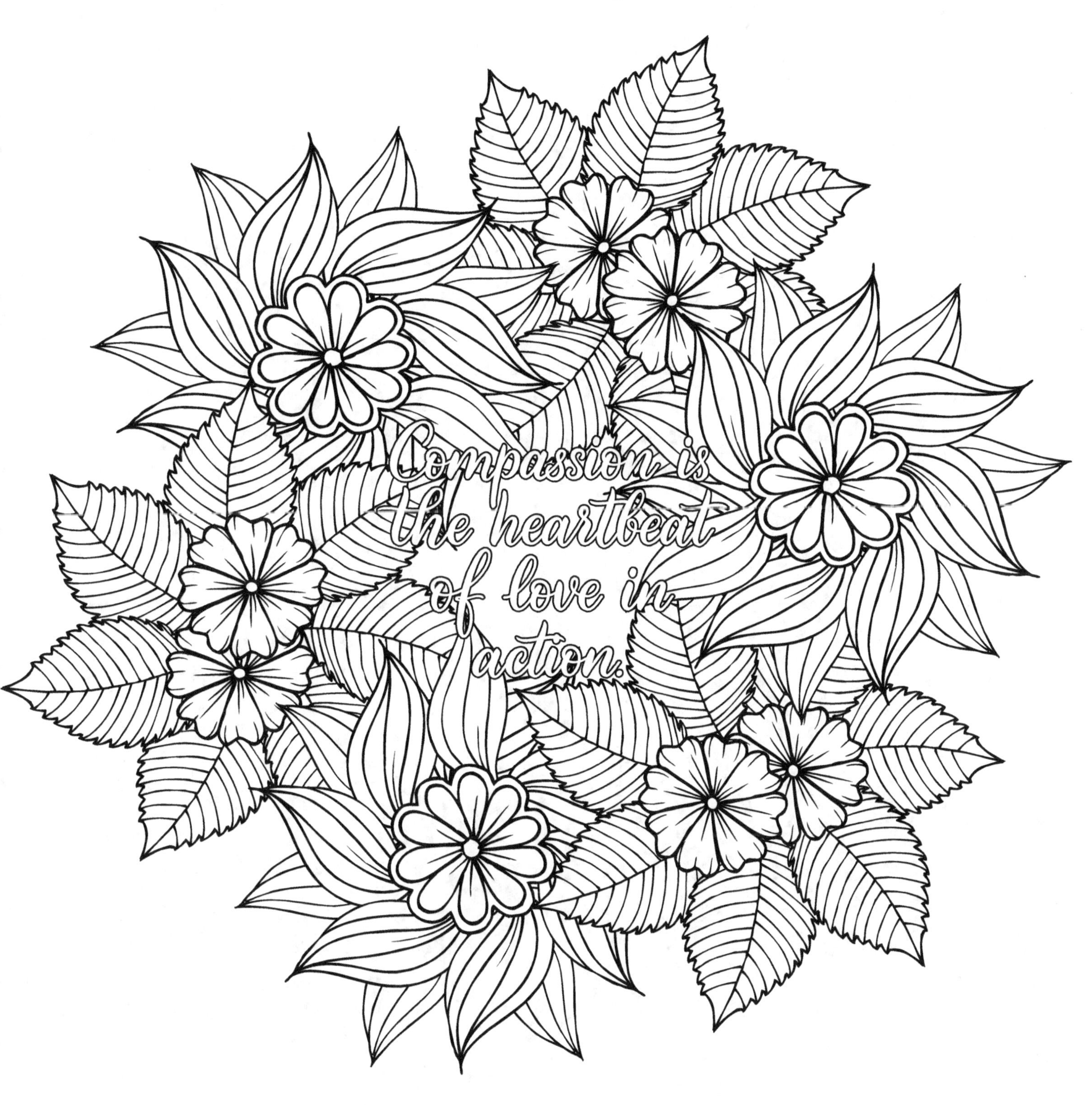

Compassion is
the heartbeat
of love in
action.

Don't be afraid to show yourself, to try things, and to feel your emotions. This is the only way to discover your inner and outer beauty. And just as in opening yourself up and being vulnerable to someone special, do not be afraid to make mistakes in the beginning, it is part of the journey.

♥ Follow the guidelines and use the blank space for practice

As you move forward to the lowercase letters, you will find that there is a great contrast in the height of the letters in this handwriting. Switching from large to small shapes is a good exercise for developing writing skills. You can also reflect on how love brings you to highs and lows, but you have to transition smoothly as you go.

♥ Follow the guidelines and use the blank space for practice

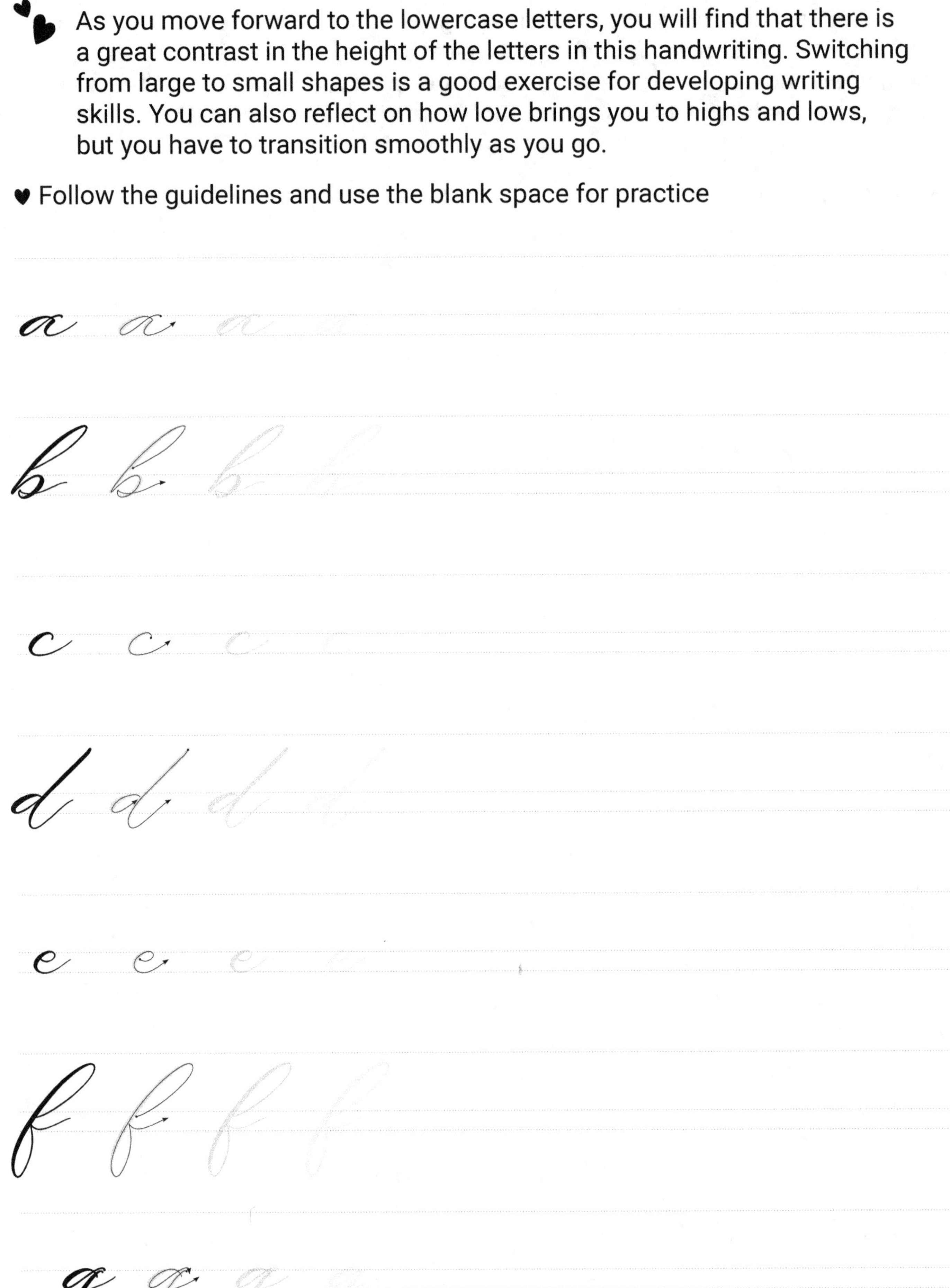

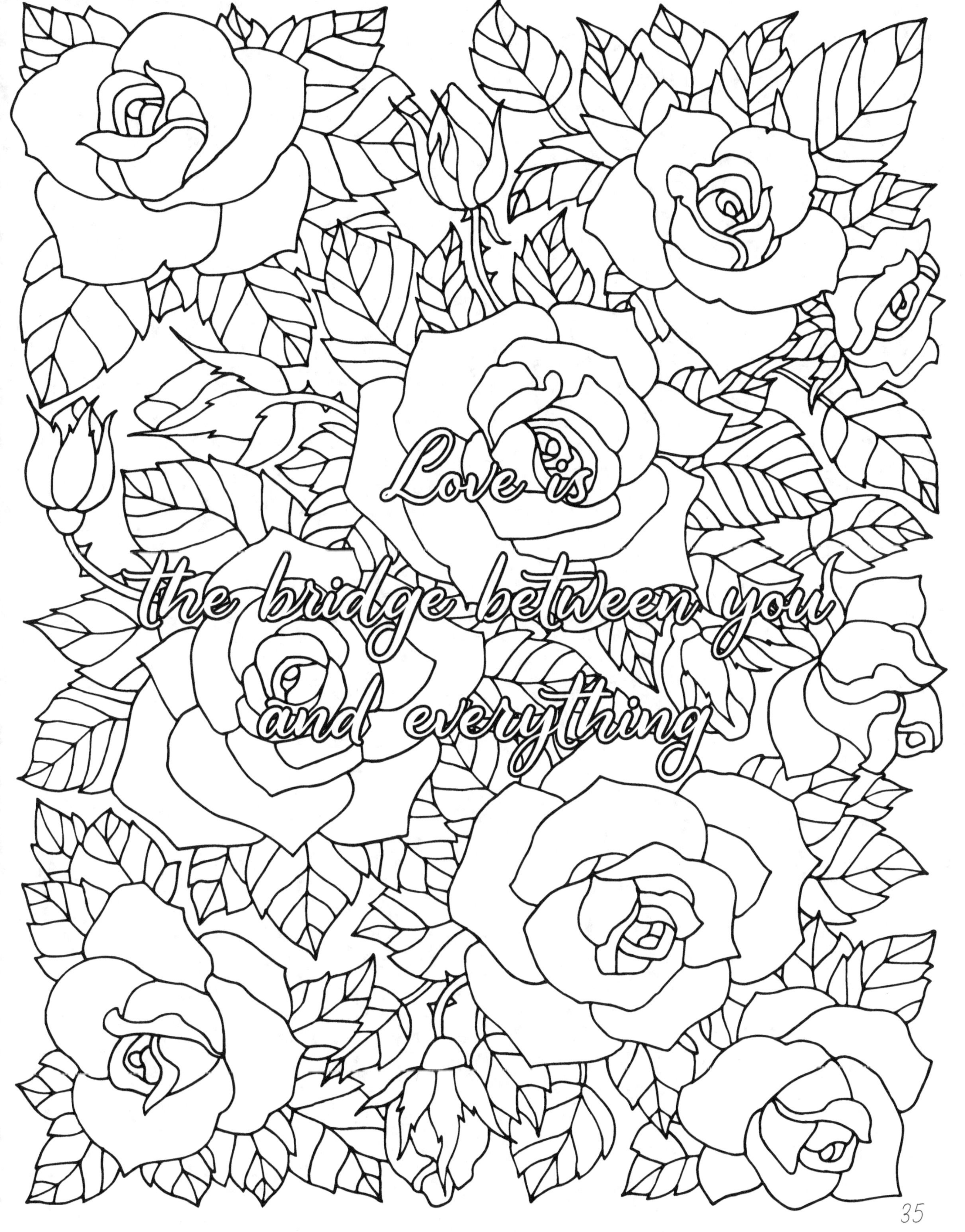

Love is
the bridge between you
and everything

Understanding and mastering the fundamental forms can significantly improve your lettering skills. It will take time and a lot of practice, but seeing the results can be worth the effort.

♥ Follow the guidelines and use the blank space for practice

Remember to celebrate your progress, no matter how small. Every line, stroke, or letter you perfect is a victory worth recognizing.

♥ Follow the guidelines and use the blank space for practice

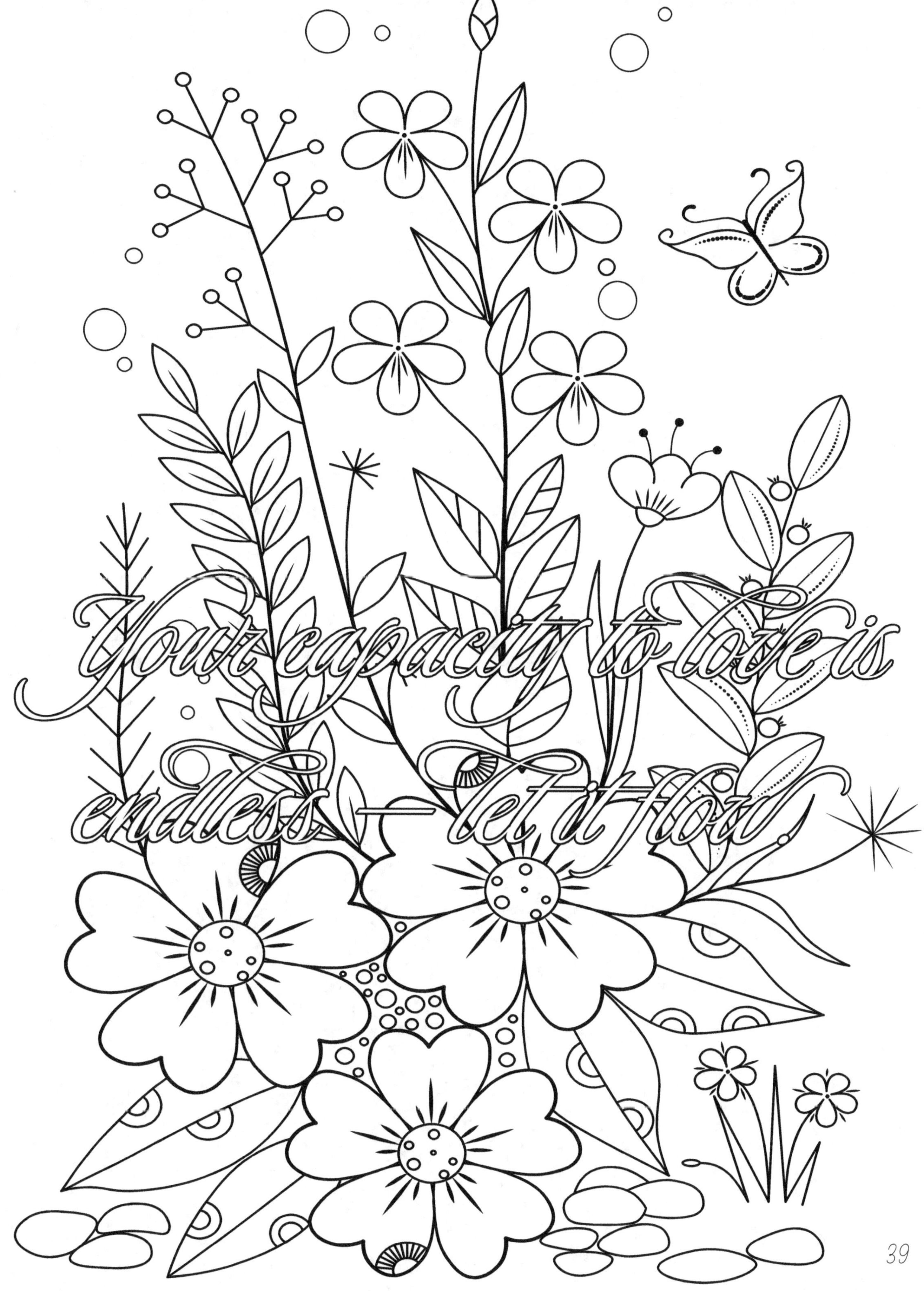
Your capacity to love is endless — let it flow

Like any other skill, practice makes perfect in lettering. Dedicate a specific time each day for lettering practice. Use the uppercase and lowercase letters you've learned to write down your reflections about how love takes time.

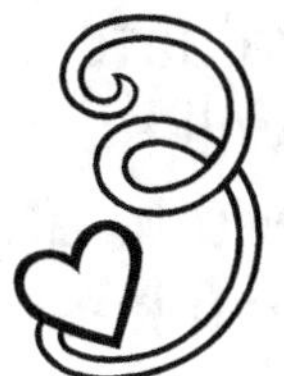

♥ Follow the guidelines and use the blank space for practice

Evaluate Your Work: After practicing, take a moment to evaluate your work. It will help you identify areas for improvement. Look for strokes that you need to adjust and control movements of your wrist when writing. Then keep practicing until you are satisfied and can show your true emotion of love through your elegant lettering.

♥ Follow the guidelines and use the blank space for practice

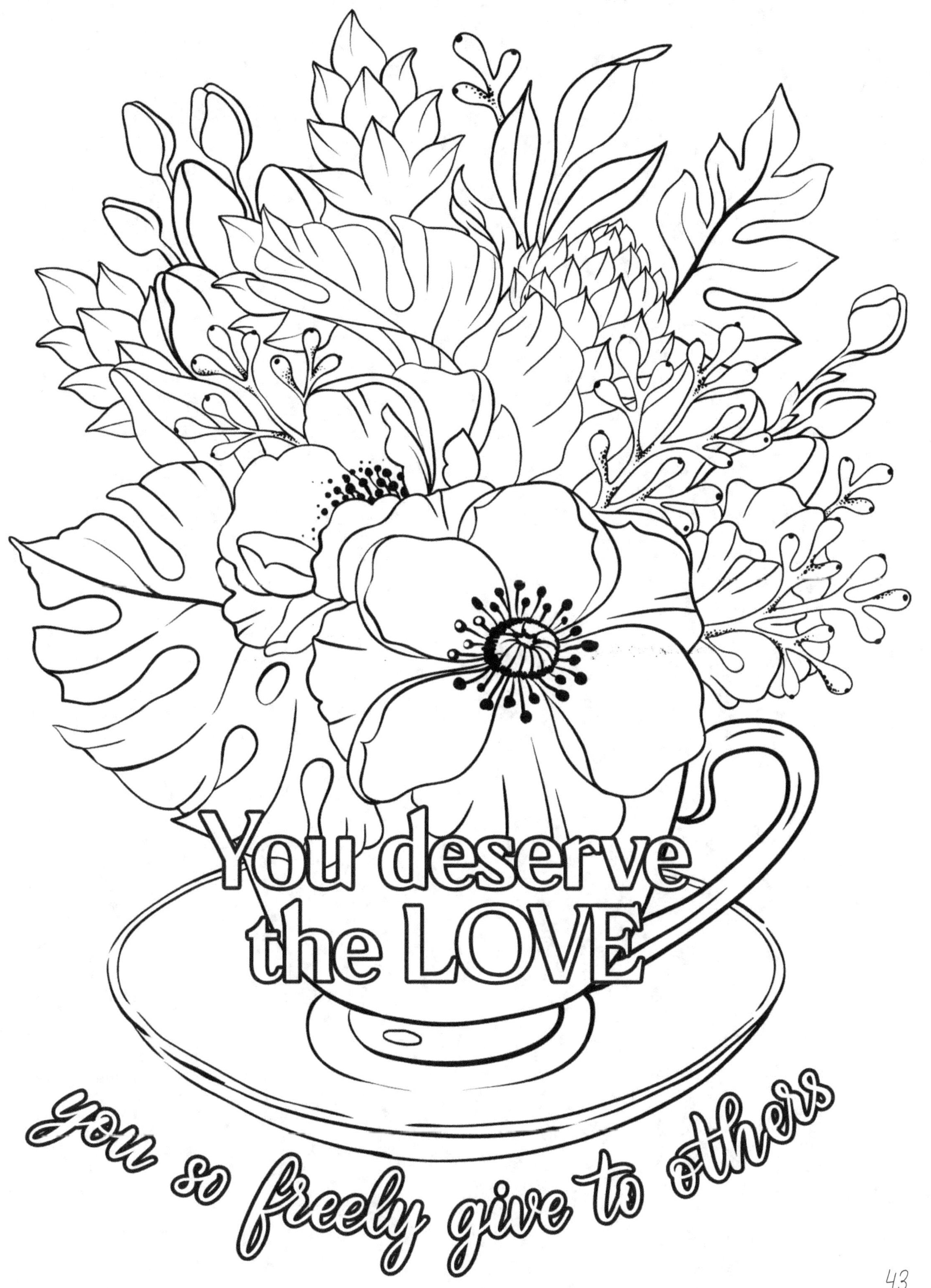

You deserve the LOVE
you so freely give to others
43

♥ Follow the guidelines and use the blank space for practice

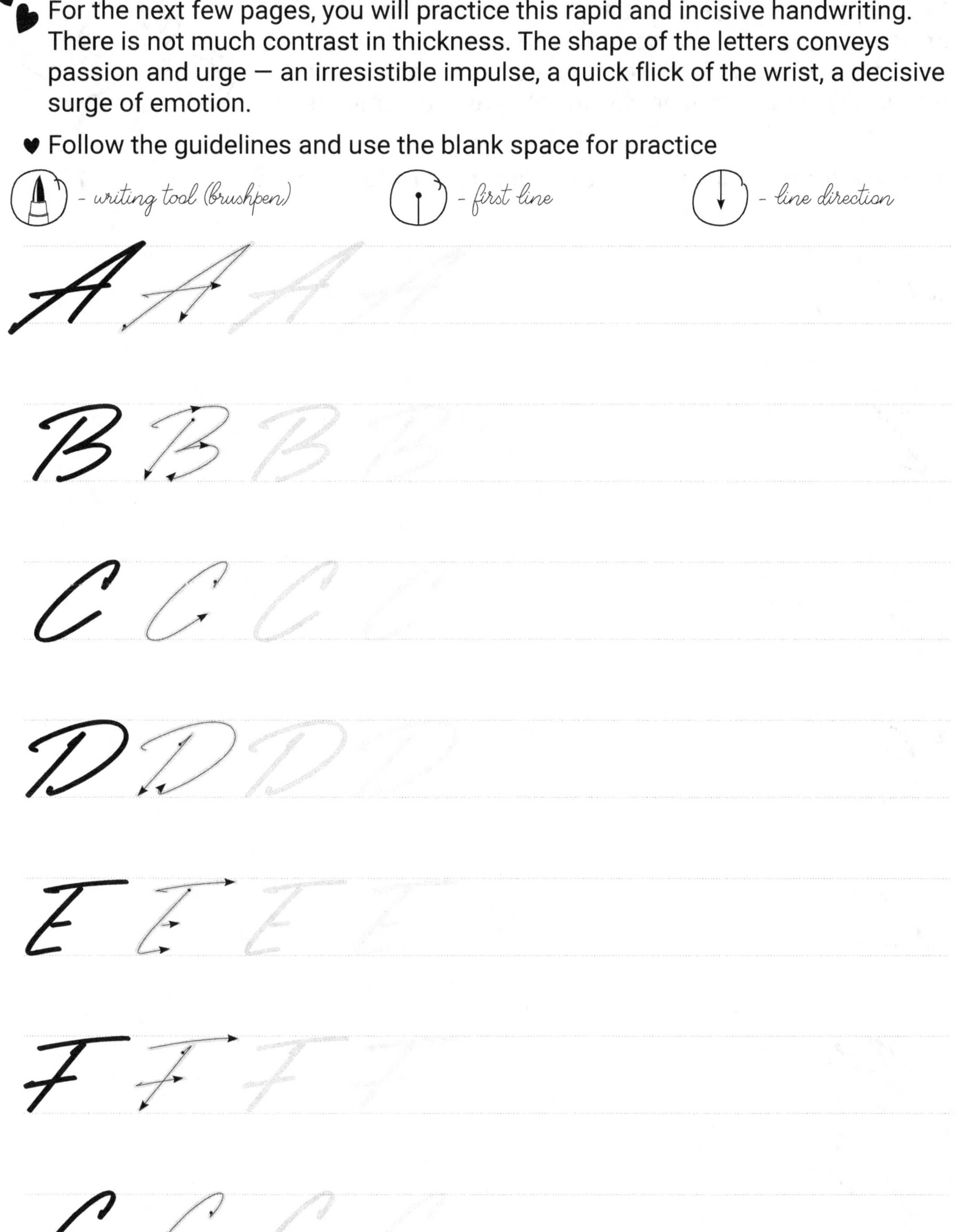

Calligraphy is an art, and like any art, it's subjective. Focus on your own journey and how far you've come. Don't compare yourself with others. You are worthy of love. You are worthy of time. You are worthy of care and compassion.

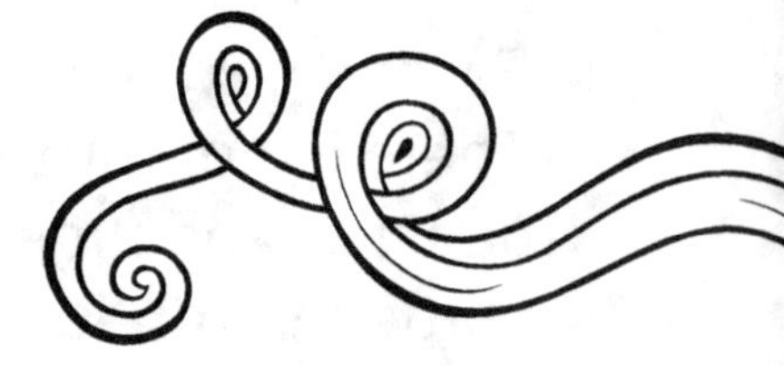

♥ Follow the guidelines and use the blank space for practice

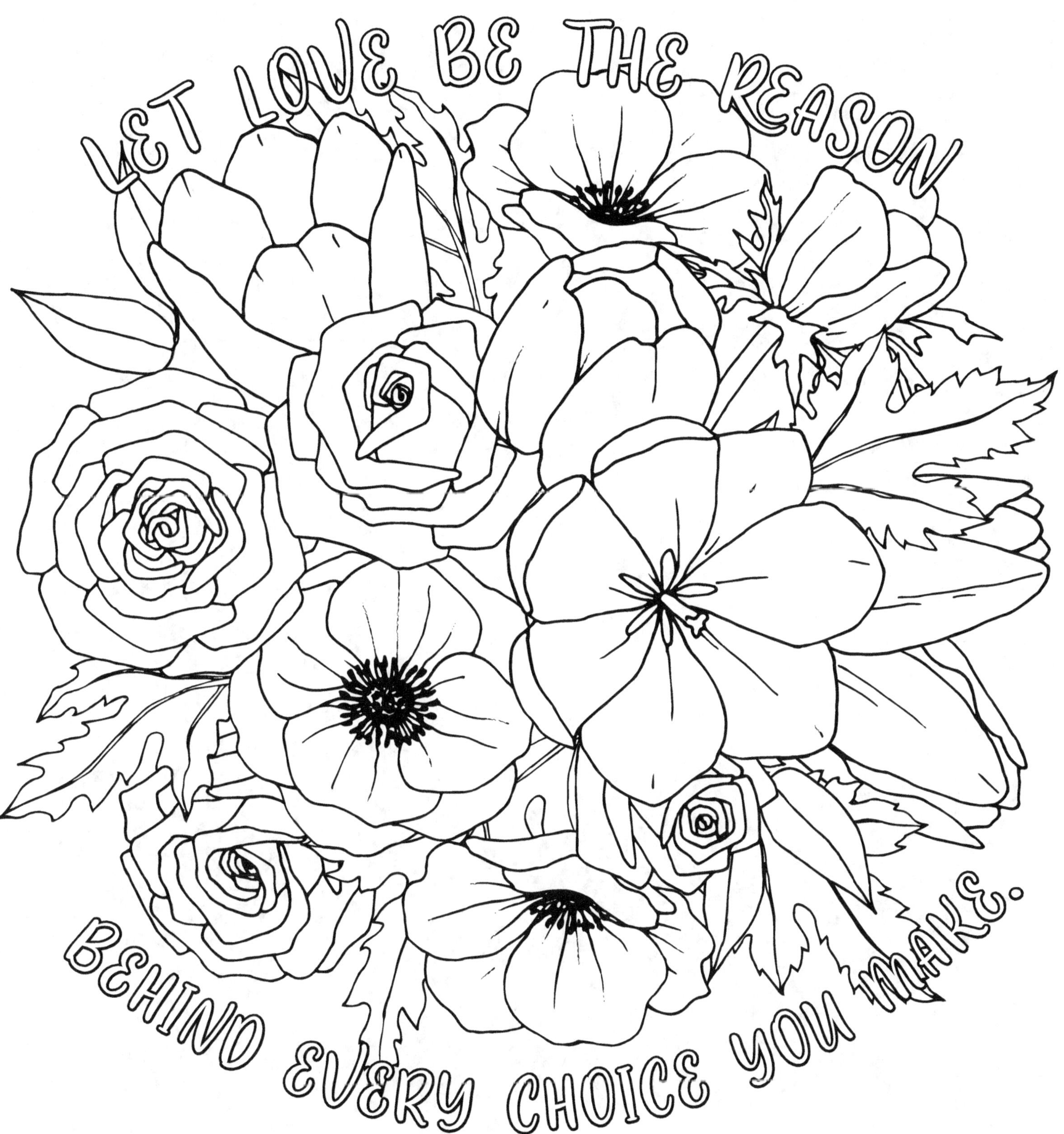

LET LOVE BE THE REASON
BEHIND EVERY CHOICE YOU MAKE.

Take time to study this particular style. See how the heavy strokes begin and end in precise marks. It conveys bravery and boldness, characteristics that make love stronger.

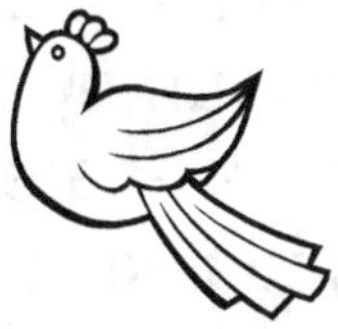

♥ Follow the guidelines and use the blank space for practice

Enjoy the process rather than focusing solely on the outcome.
The journey of beautiful writing is like the journey of self-love
and self-care. It doesn't happen overnight, but as you continue
practicing and showing acceptance of yourself, you bloom into
a beautiful version of the person you truly are.

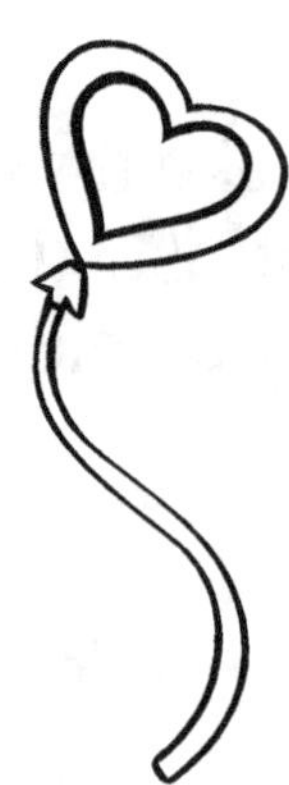

♥ Follow the guidelines and use the blank space for practice

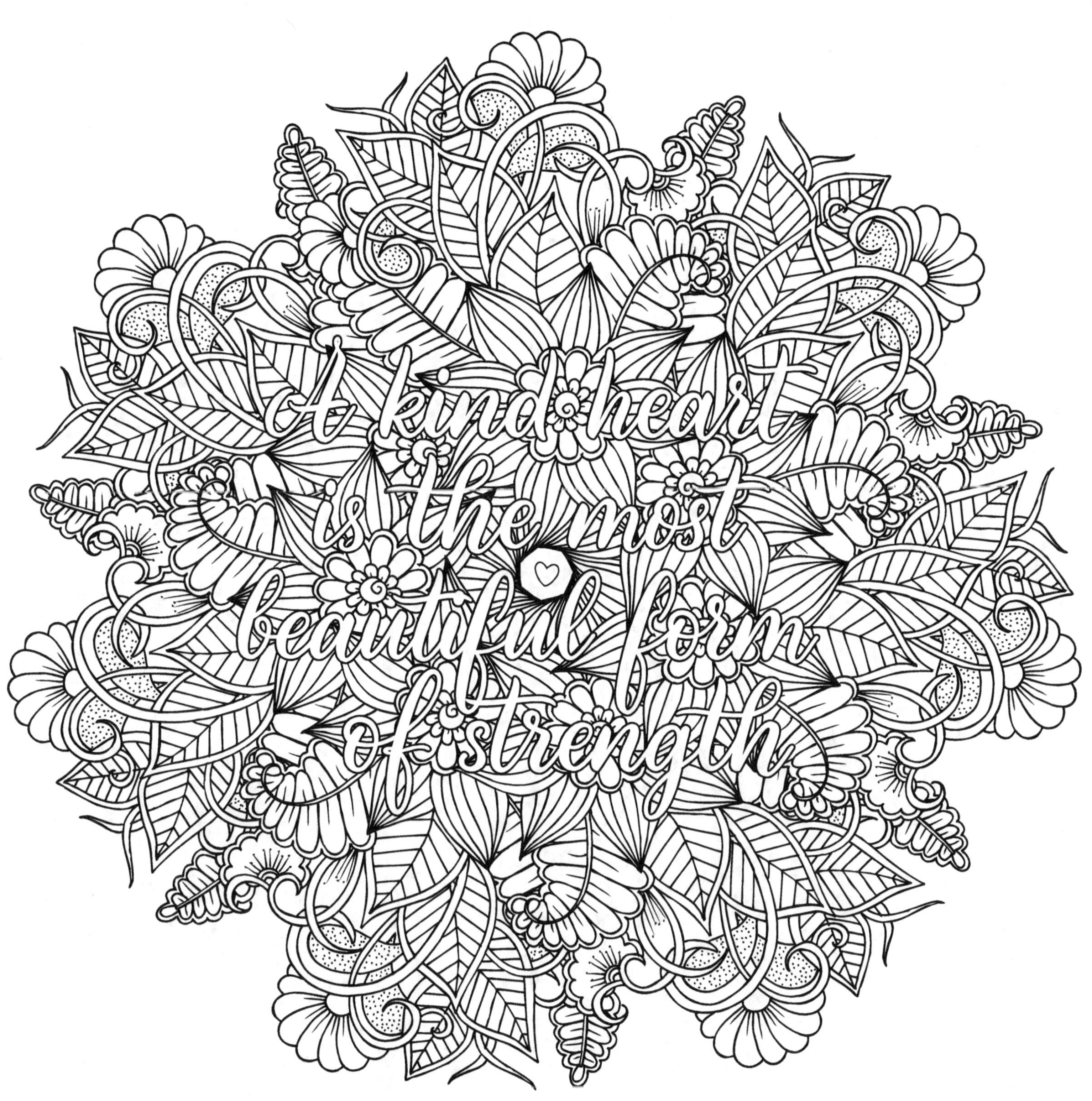

A kind heart
is the most
beautiful form
of strength

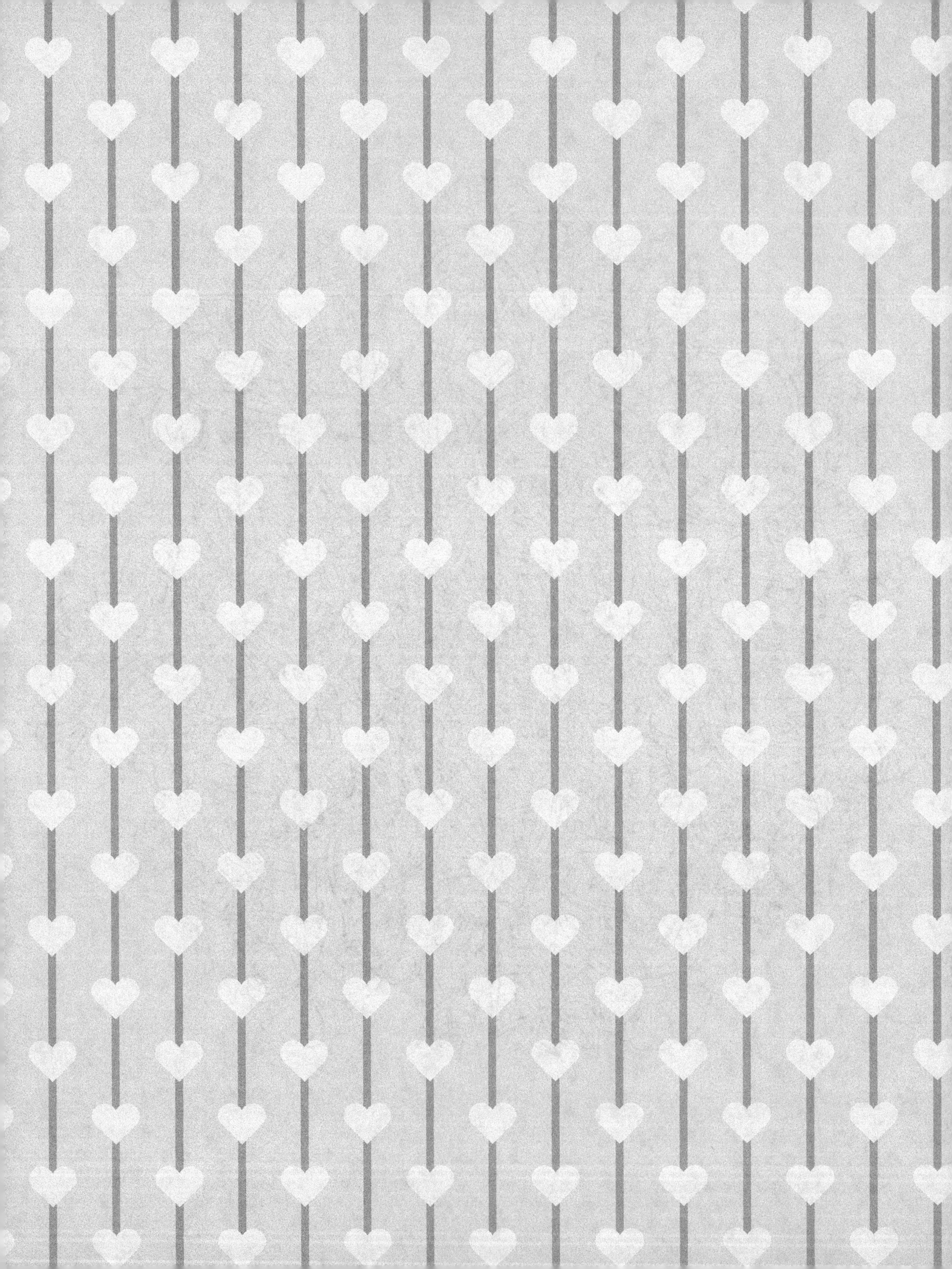

Don't rush the process. Be patient with yourself and enjoy the learning process. You are now moving forward to the lowercase letters. Though they are short and quicker to write, they have equal importance with uppercase letters. You need both to express emotions through words and lettering.

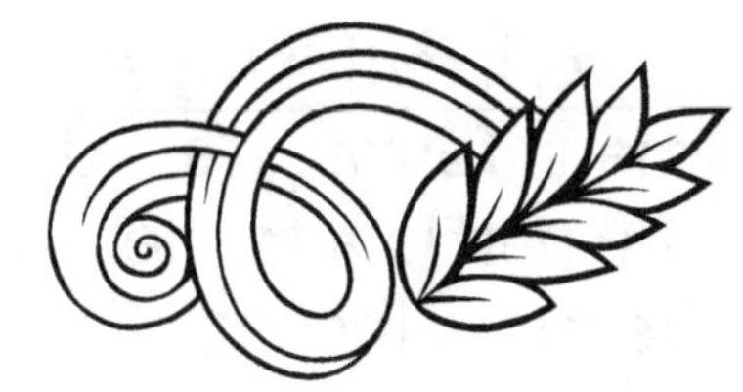

♥ Follow the guidelines and use the blank space for practice

Love, like the most exquisite piece of art, is open to interpretation and takes many forms. It's a dance of the heart, a symphony of feelings. Every stroke of the pen is a tender touch, and every color is a different emotion. Think of your heart as the artist's palette, and your feelings as the vibrant colors, each one unique yet harmoniously blending.

♥ Follow the guidelines and use the blank space for practice

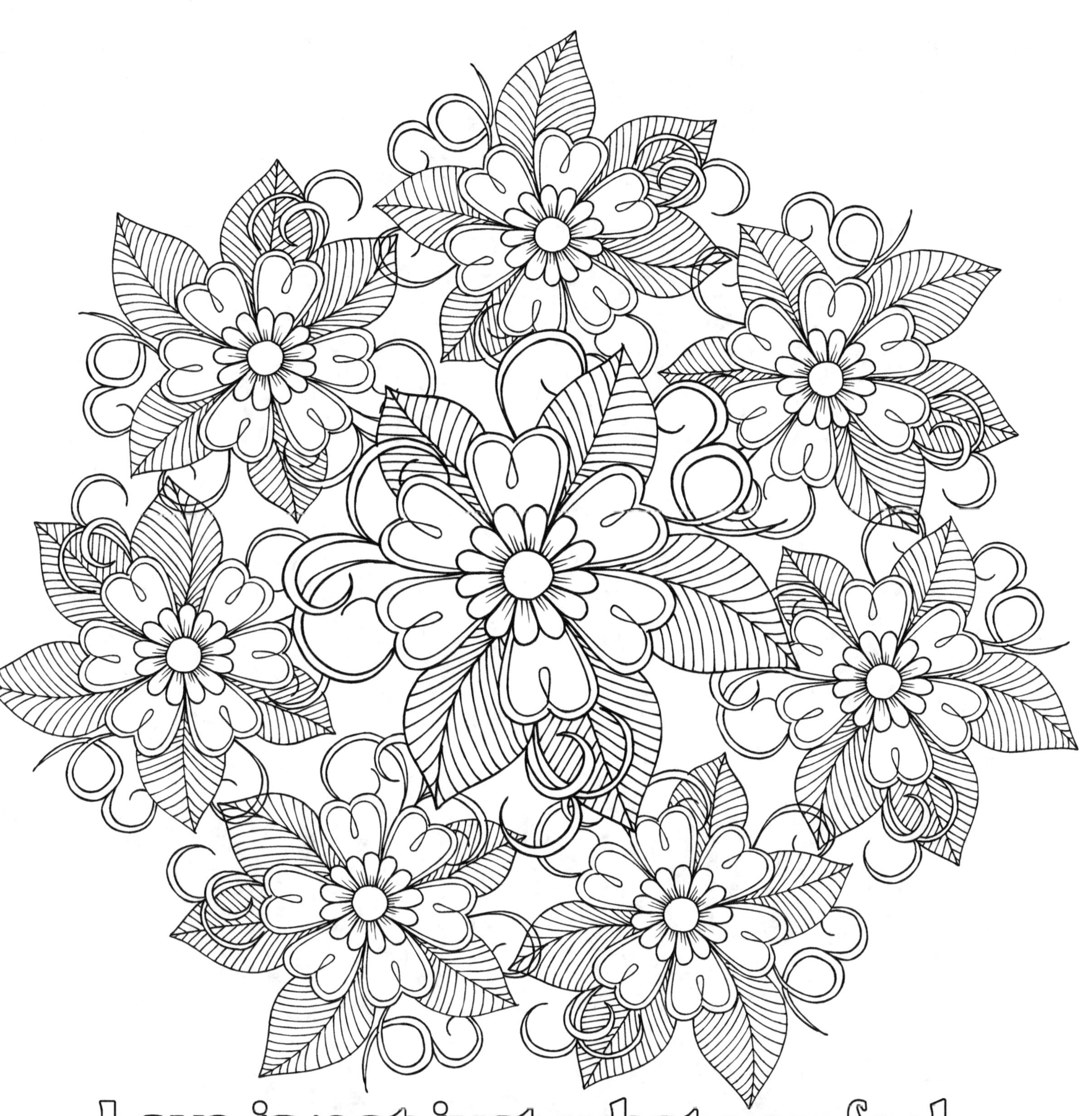

Love is not just what you feel.
It's what you do!

Remember, the act of creating is in itself, a form of self-love. Think of all the times you showed yourself care and compassion—you created something in yourself that no one else can: it's a close relationship with who you truly are, a relationship that belongs solely to you.

♥ Follow the guidelines and use the blank space for practice

Love is not something that can be contained in words alone, it's an ever-evolving thing, constantly transforming and changing with each passing moment. Whether it's the passion of a grand love affair or the tenderness of a close friendship, all forms of love are equally beautiful and special. Think about the kind of love you're writing about now - patient, kind, and gentle, or maybe passionate and bold.

♥ Follow the guidelines and use the blank space for practice

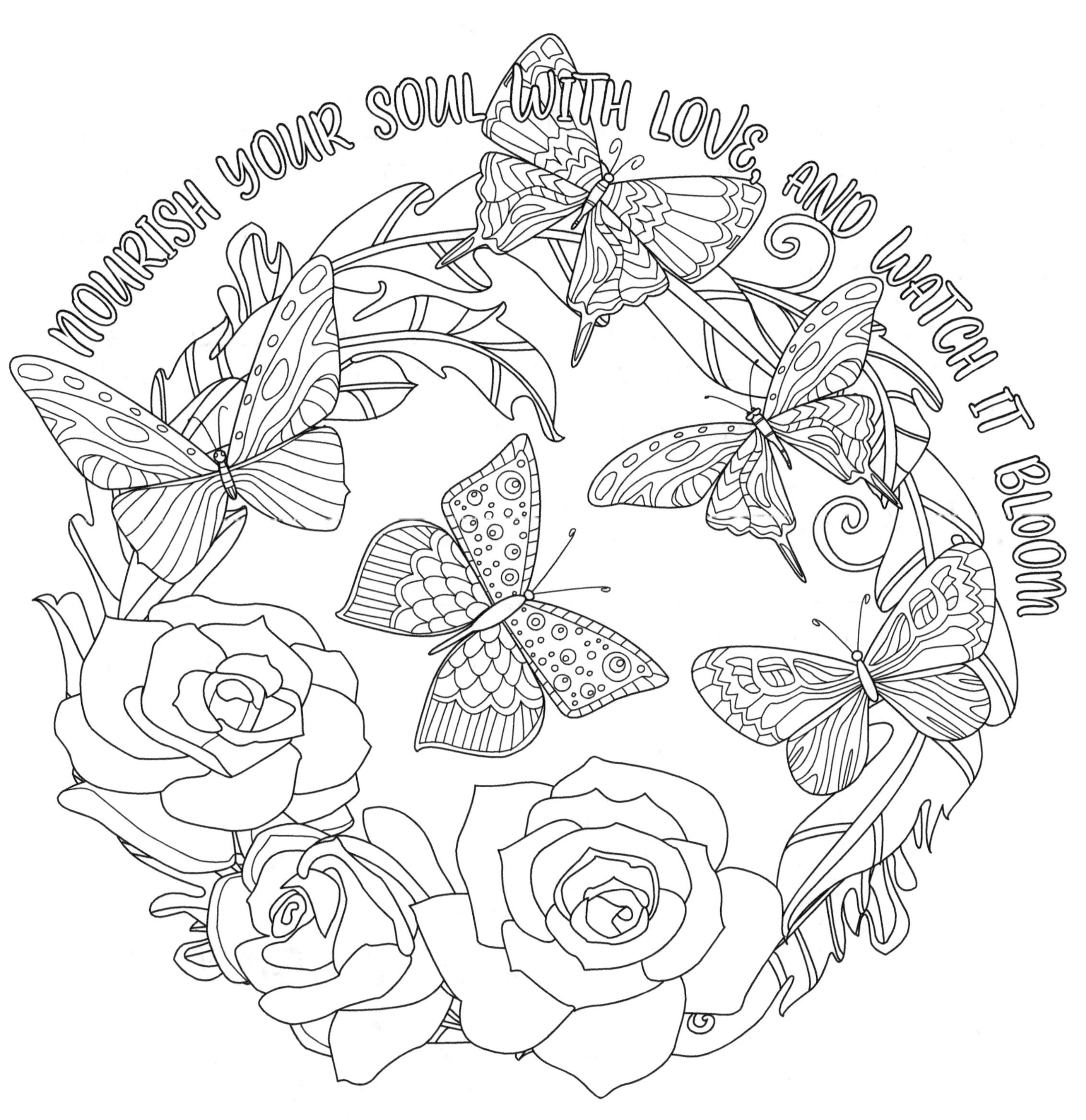

NOURISH YOUR SOUL WITH LOVE, AND WATCH IT BLOOM

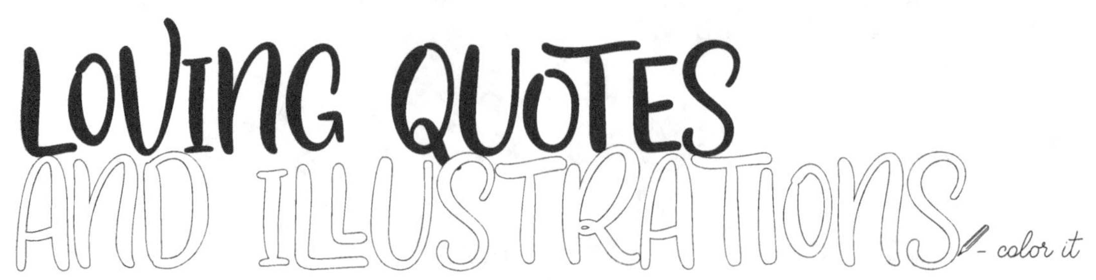

♥ Now that you have explored new styles of calligraphy and exercised your creativity in practicing these styles, it's time to combine these letters into loving quotes and affirmations. When you read these quotes, reflect on what they mean to you. Do the quotes bring a memory to your mind? Do they make you feel seen, heard, and even loved? Let these reflections be expressed in the way you create your own composition.

Use the pages to practice the quote. Write it several times until you are satisfied and you believe what the quote says. Create your own composition with each quote.

Where there is love there is life.

Where there is Love there is Life

WHERE THERE IS

Love

Love

THERE IS LIFE

Love

WHERE THERE IS

Love

THERE IS

Life

Where there is
LOVE
there is life

♥ Love can complete you. A person who has love finds more things to be grateful for and not just in material things but also in relationships. If you have love, your limits are endless.

All we need is love

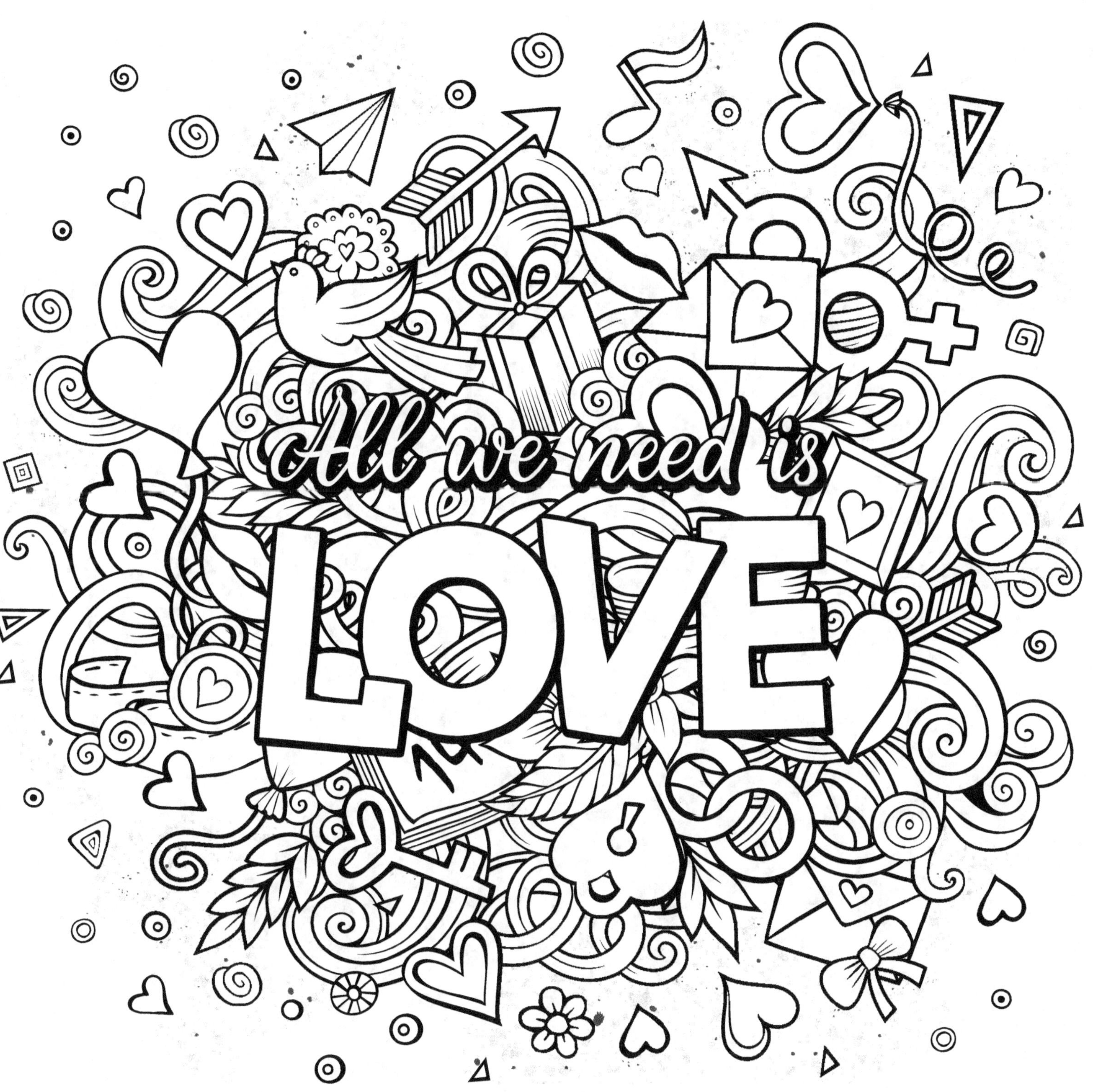

All we need is
LOVE

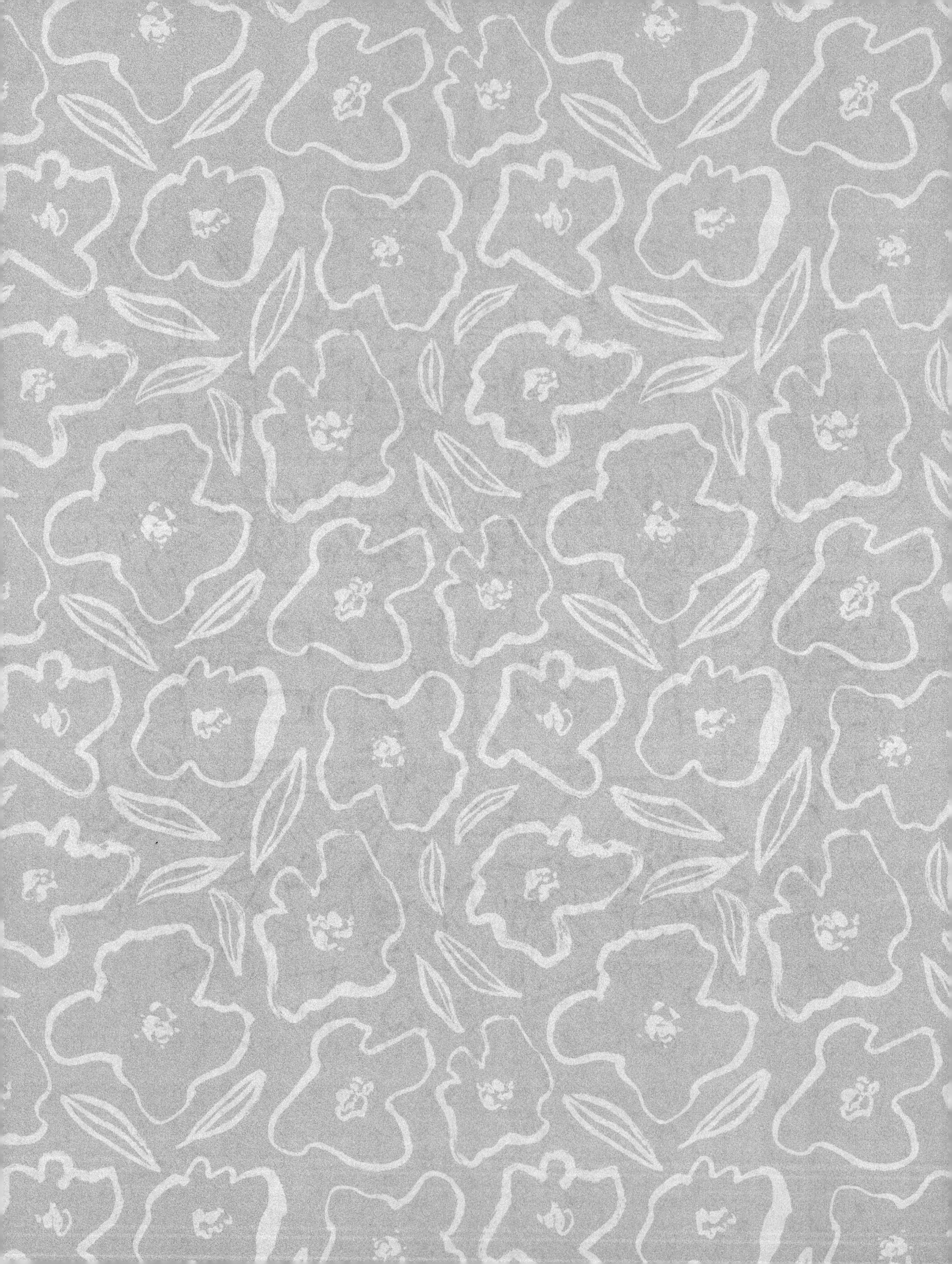

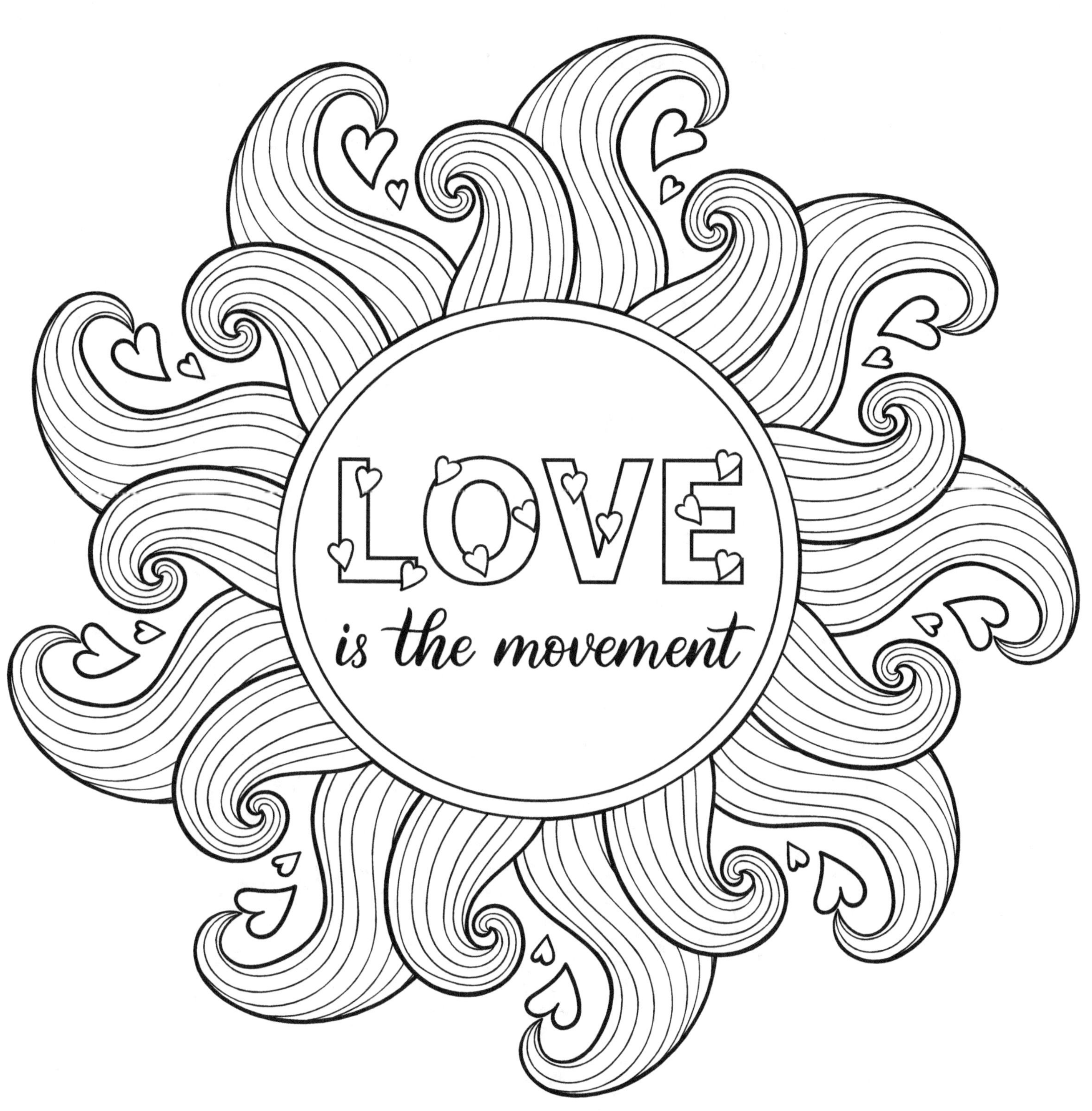
LOVE
is the movement

♥ There is freedom in love and being vulnerable and transparent to the one you love is the lightest feeling. Have you found the one who loves you without judgment? Do you love yourself without any judgment?

Love is the absence of judgment

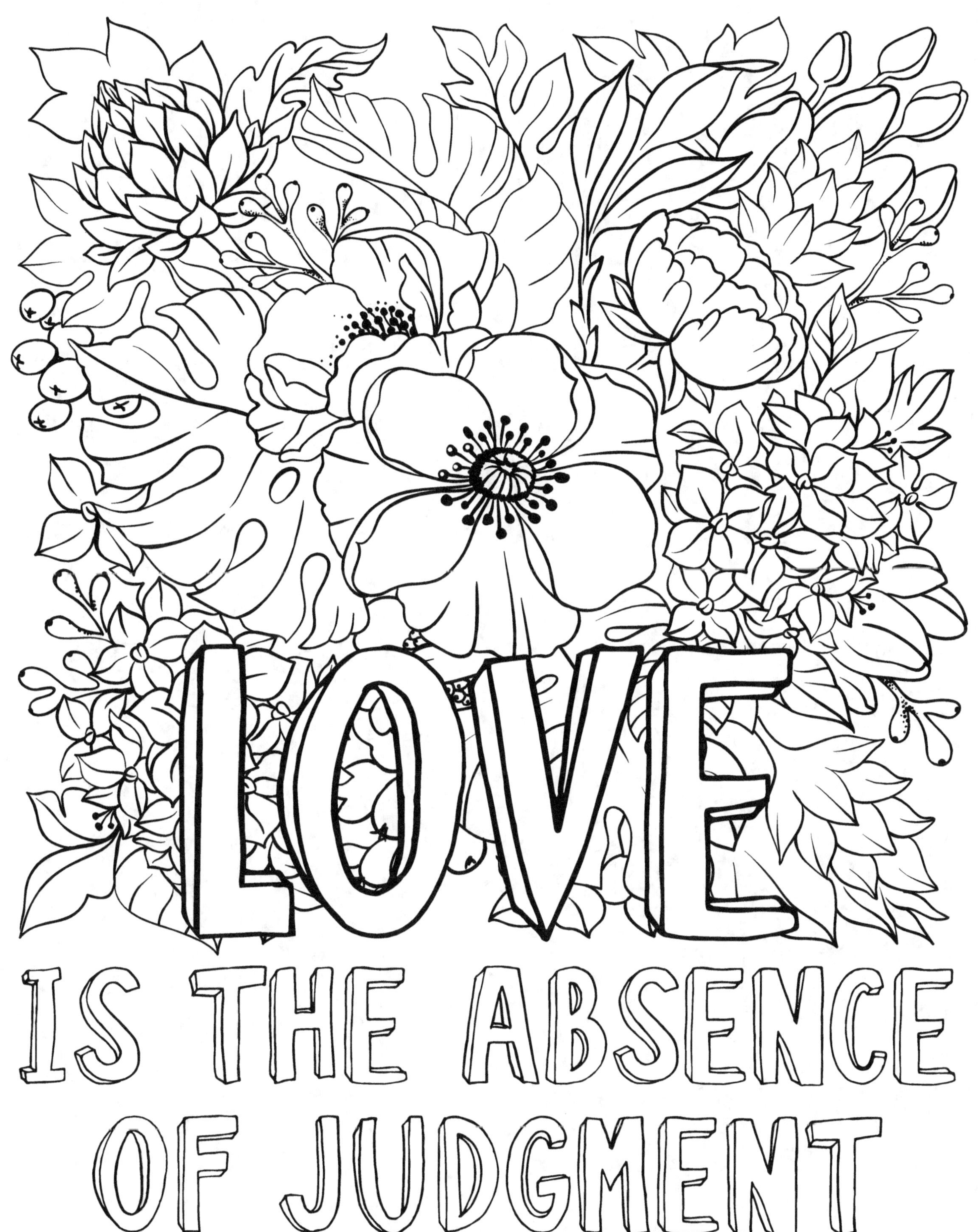

LOVE
IS THE ABSENCE
OF JUDGMENT

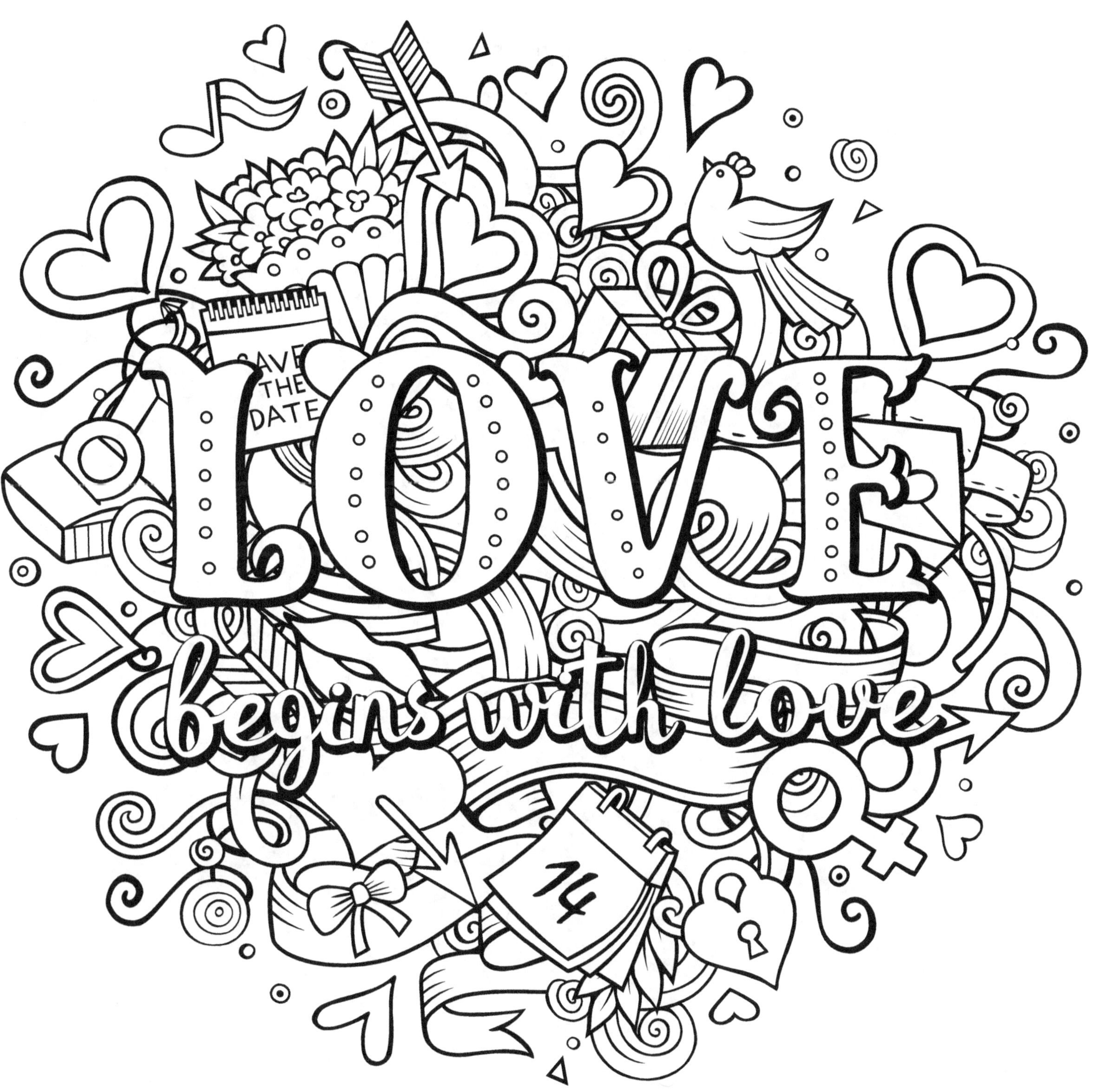

SAVE THE DATE
LOVE
begins with love
14

♥ They say that beauty is in the eye of the beholder. Well, love is the beauty of the soul. Everyone who shows love shines as a beautiful person. Your best beauty regimen is not skin deep but it is to learn to love yourself and others.

Love is the beauty of soul

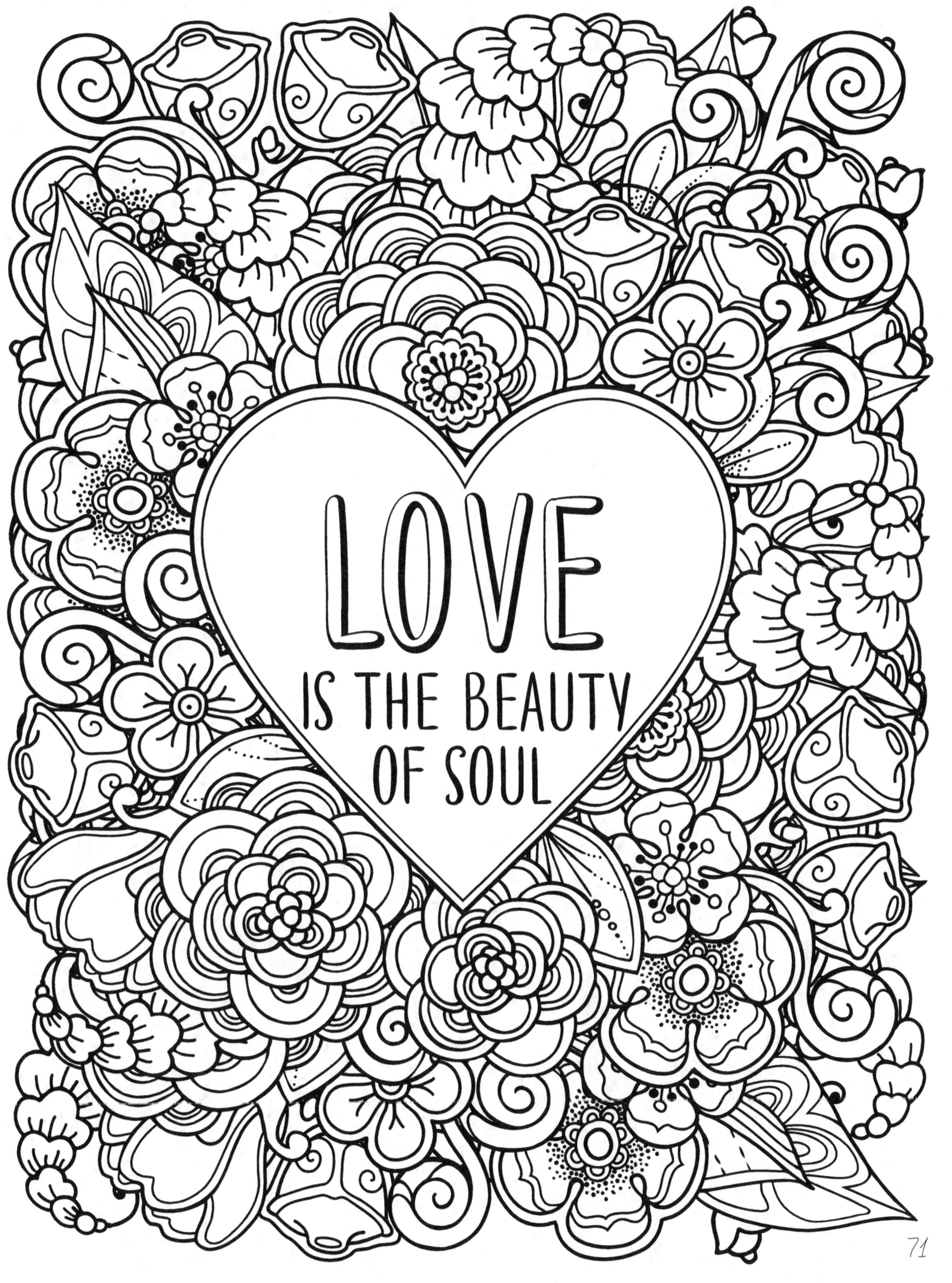

LOVE
IS THE BEAUTY
OF SOUL

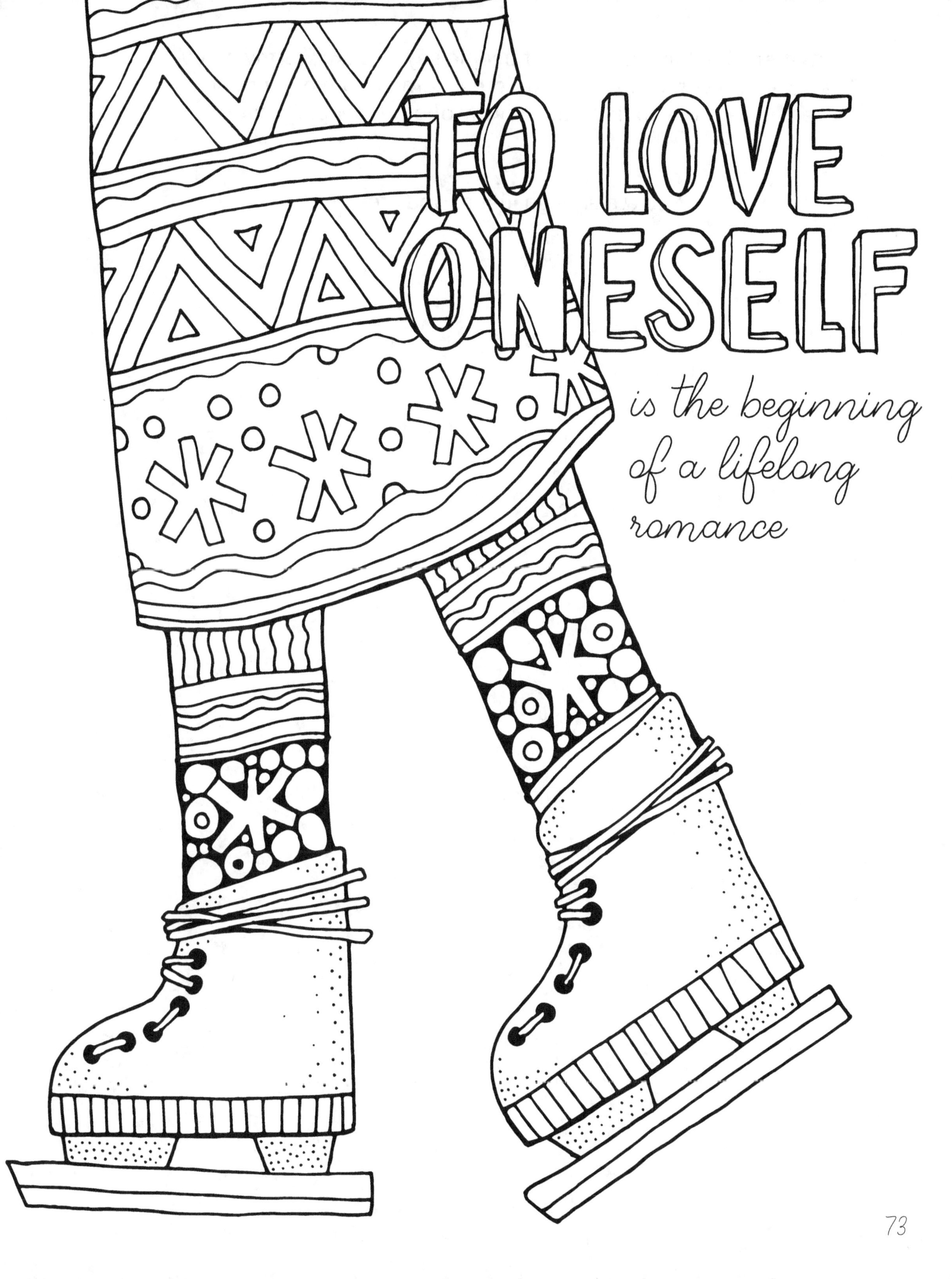

TO LOVE ONESELF
is the beginning
of a lifelong
romance

♥ No matter what happens or what people say, you are worthy of love.
That love first comes from you before it comes from other people.
You are worthy of your love and worthy of other people's love.

You are enough just as you are

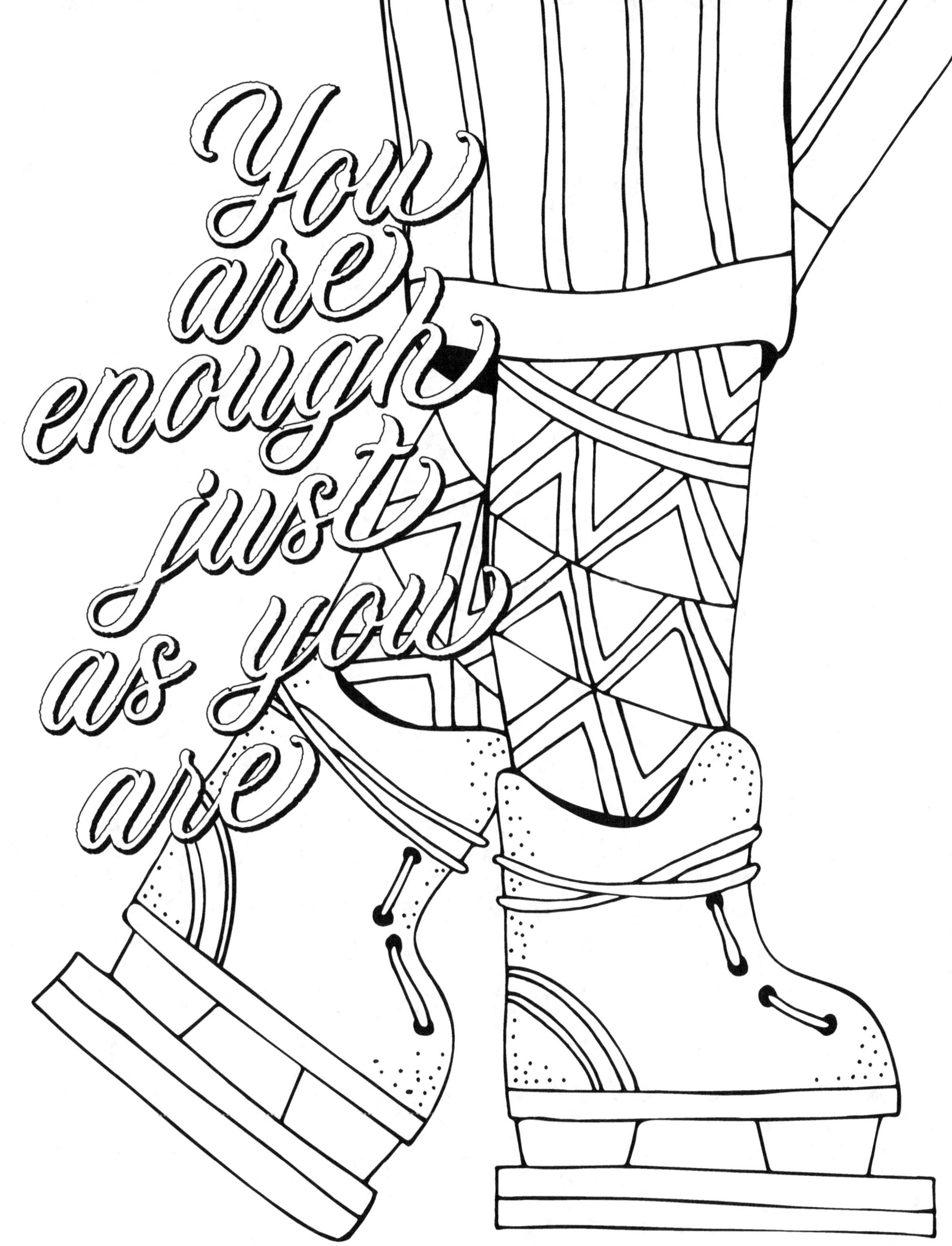

You are enough just as you are

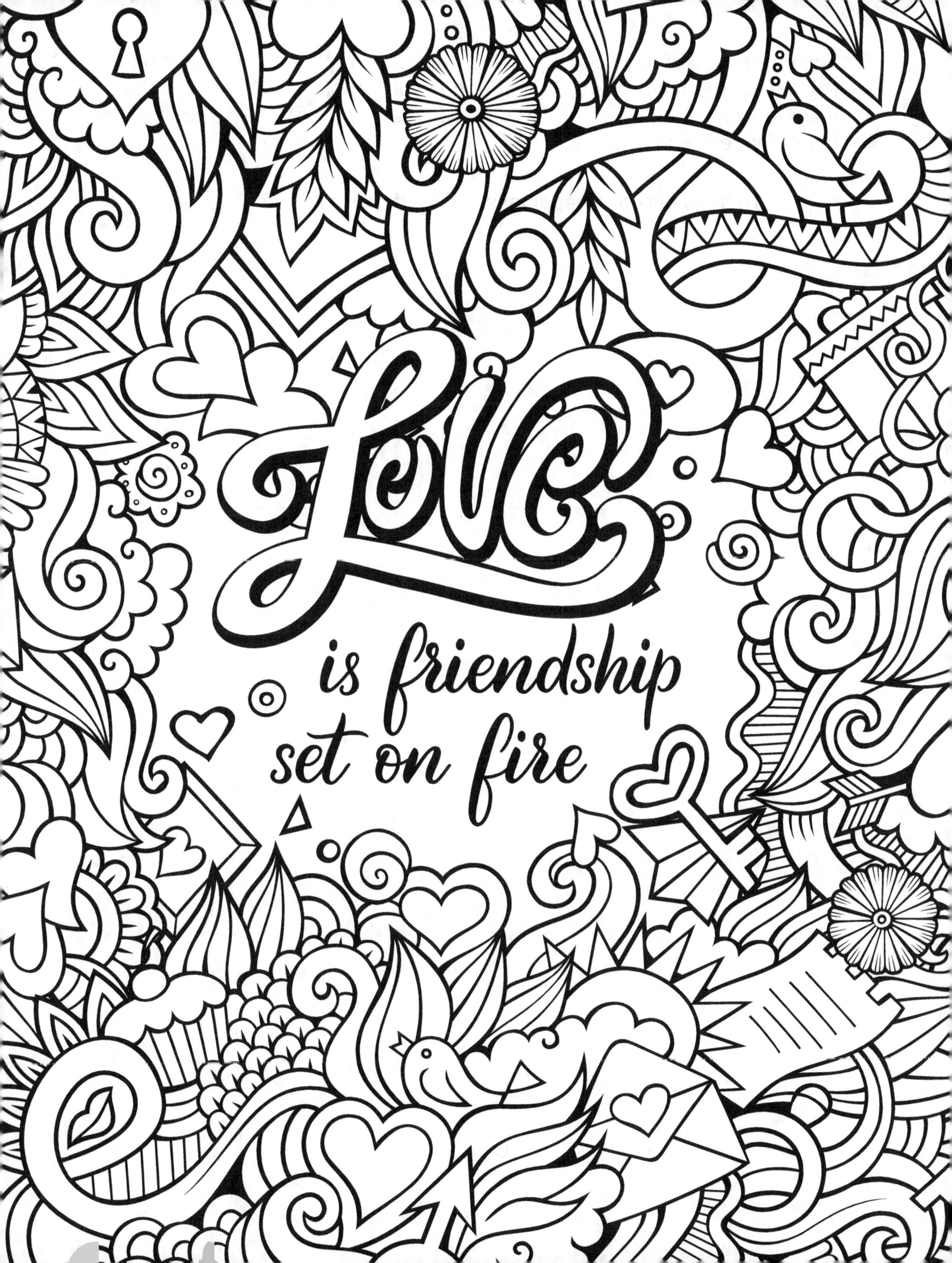

Love
is friendship
set on fire

♥ The emptiness of days can be attributed to the emptiness of love. When you love something or someone, it brings you happiness. When was the last time you said "I love you"? When was the last time you showed love to someone or to yourself?

There is only one happiness in this life, to love and be loved

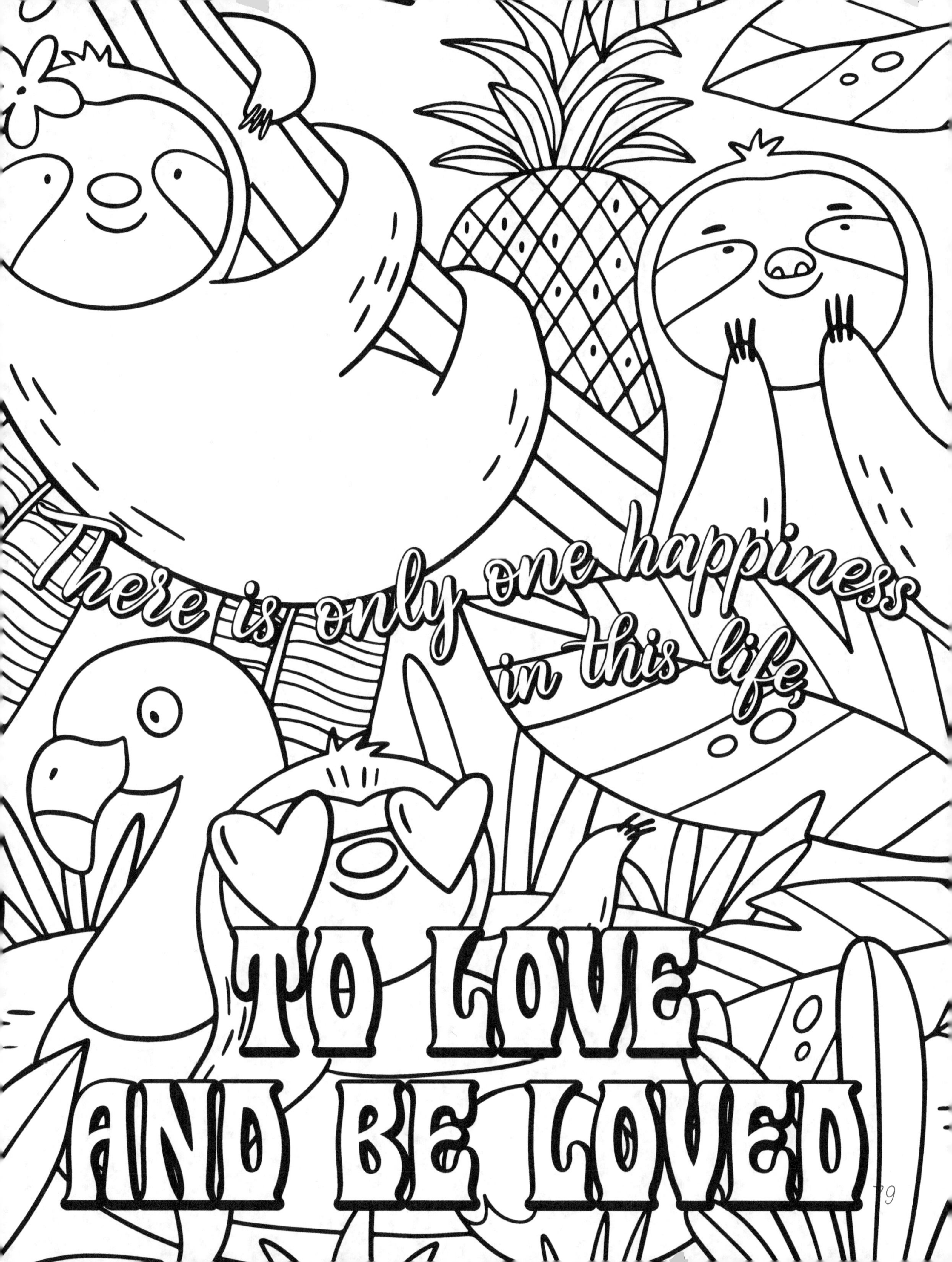

There is only one happiness in this life,
TO LOVE AND BE LOVED

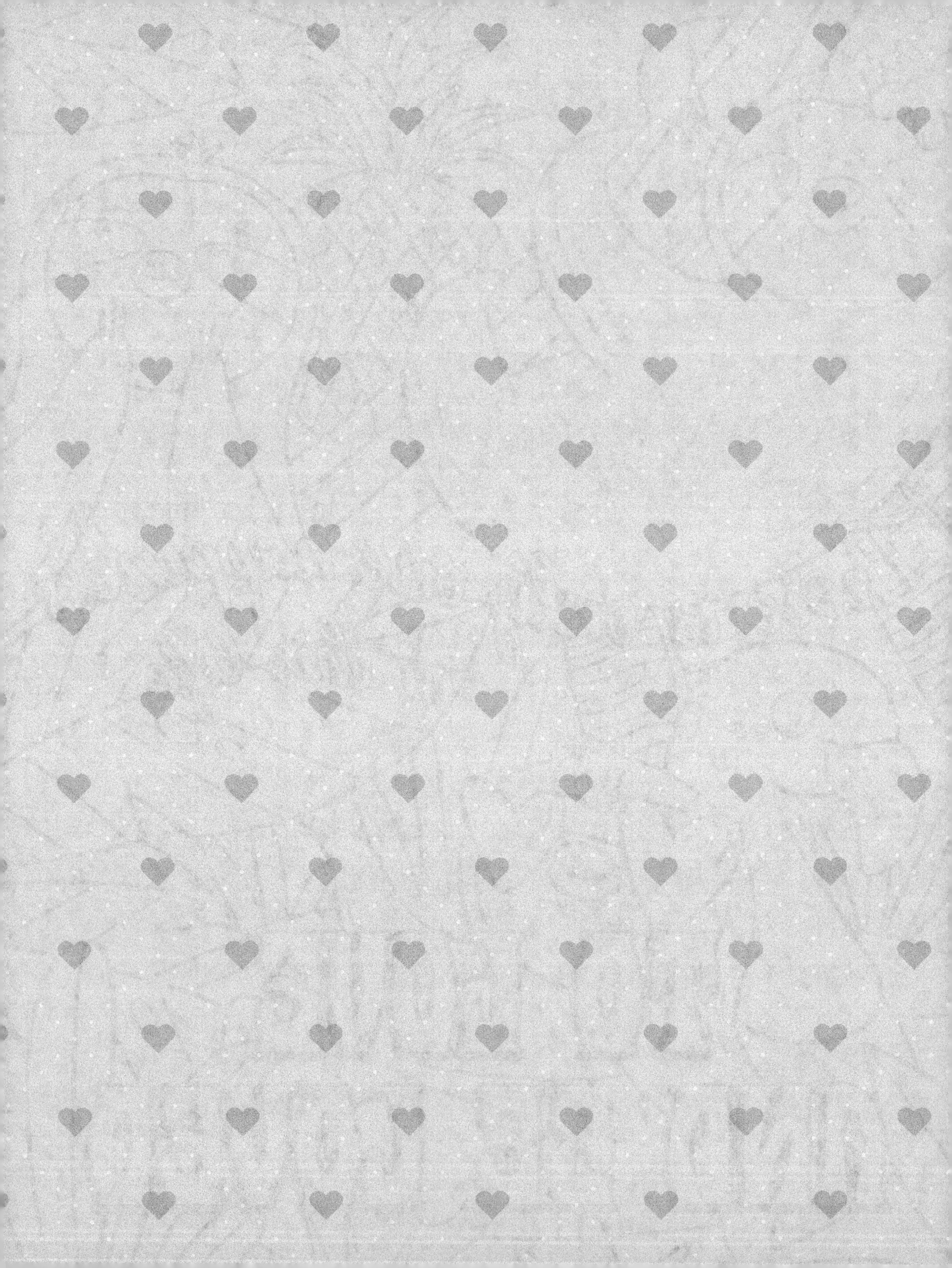

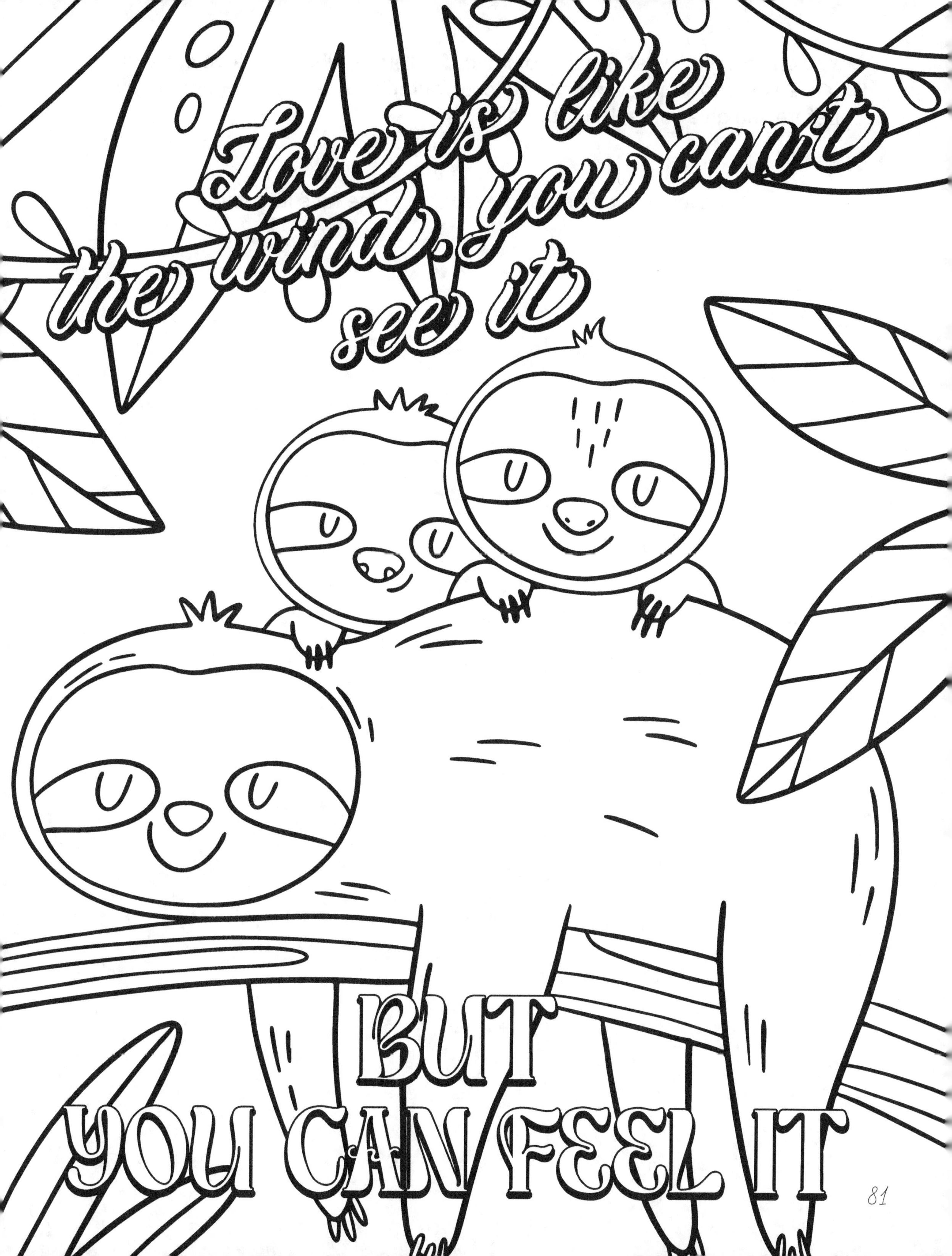

Love is like the wind, you can't see it
BUT
YOU CAN FEEL IT

♥ You cannot give what you do not have. Therefore, when you love someone, it is an overflow of how much you love yourself. Give yourself enough love before you give yourself to others.

Love yourself first and everything else falls into line

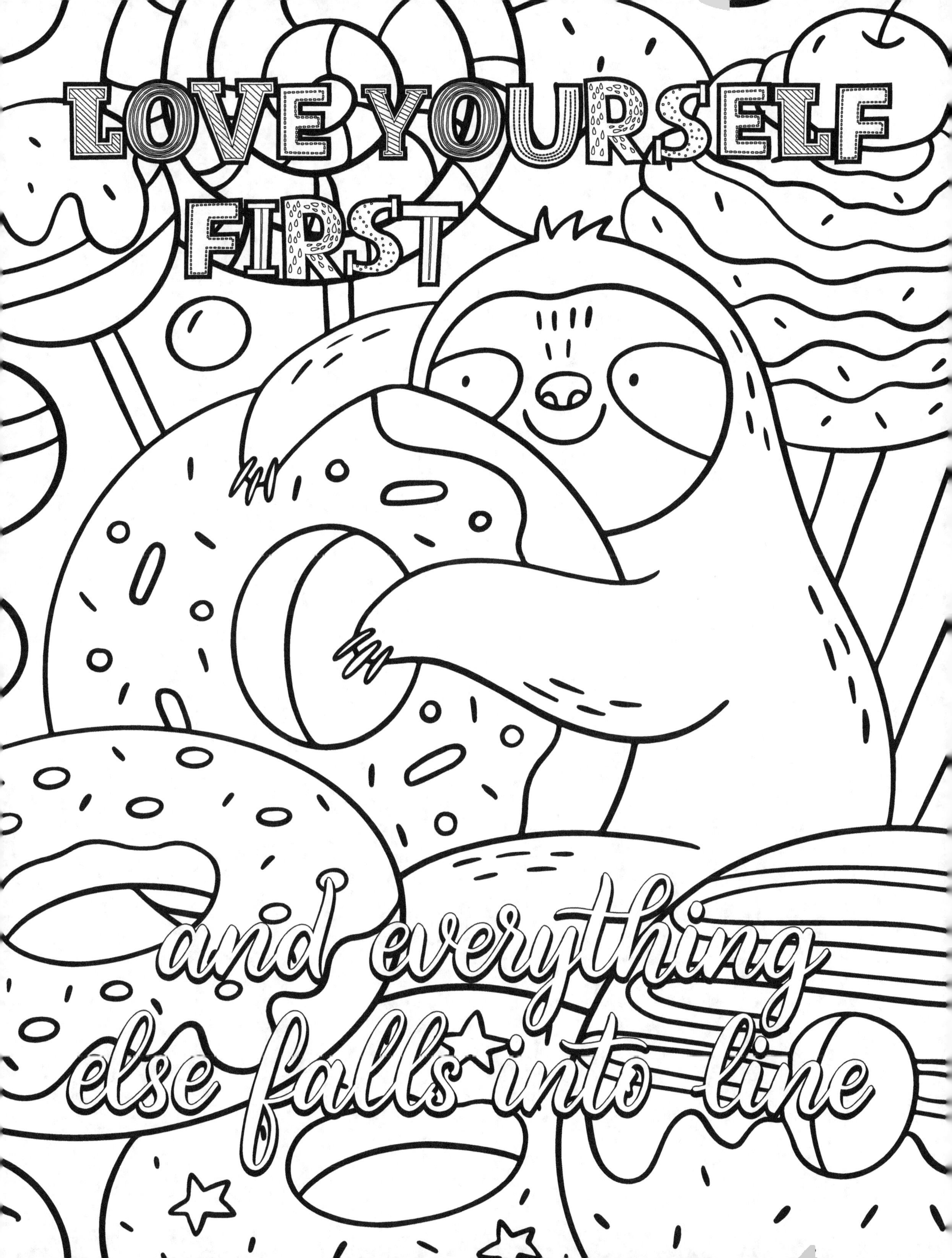

LOVE YOURSELF FIRST
and everything else falls into line

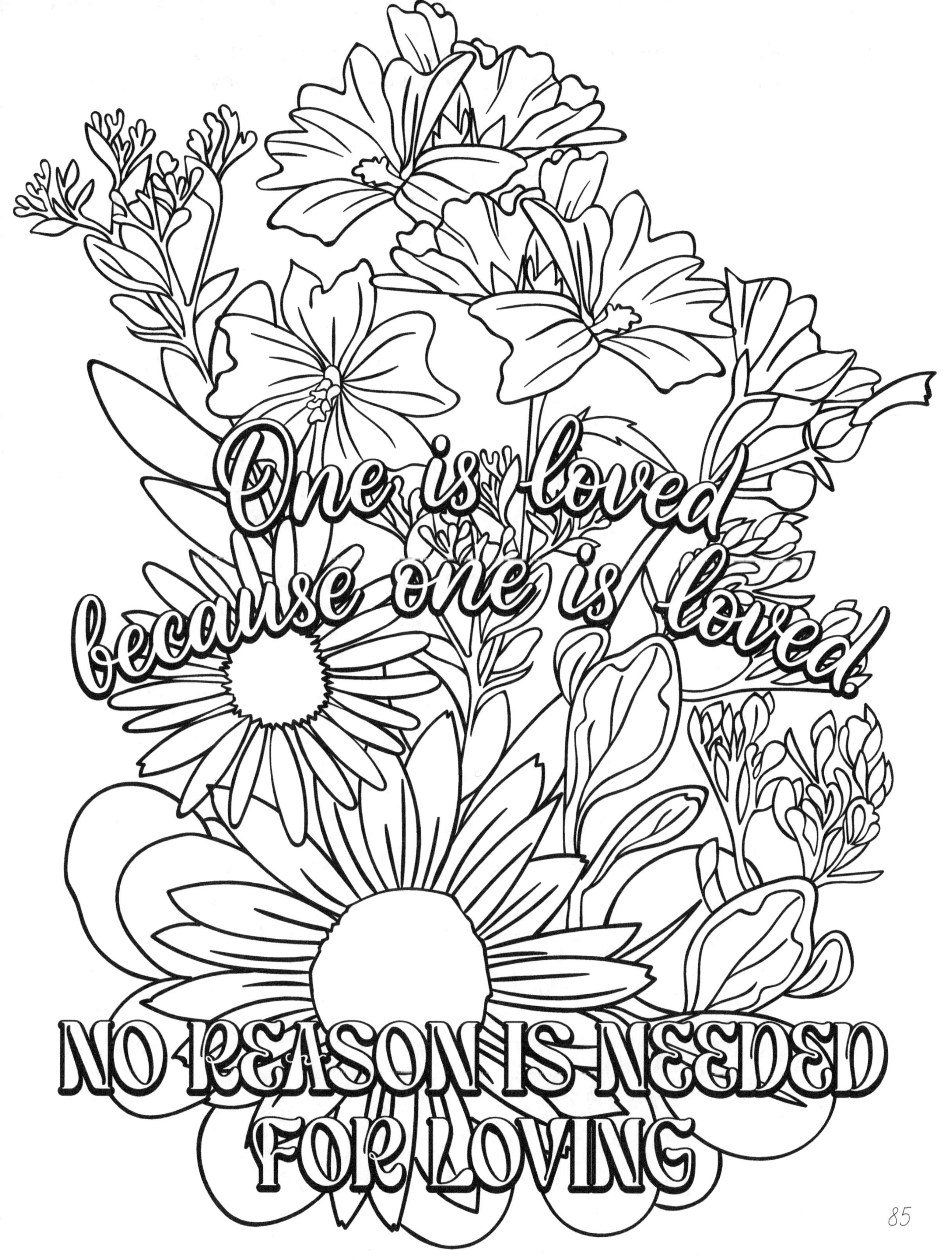

One is loved
because one is loved
NO REASON IS NEEDED
FOR LOVING

♥ Love is a choice. Love only ends when you choose to end it. It is a beautiful thing to have a love that lasts a lifetime. Choose to love.

One lifelong love

ONE LIFELONG LOVE

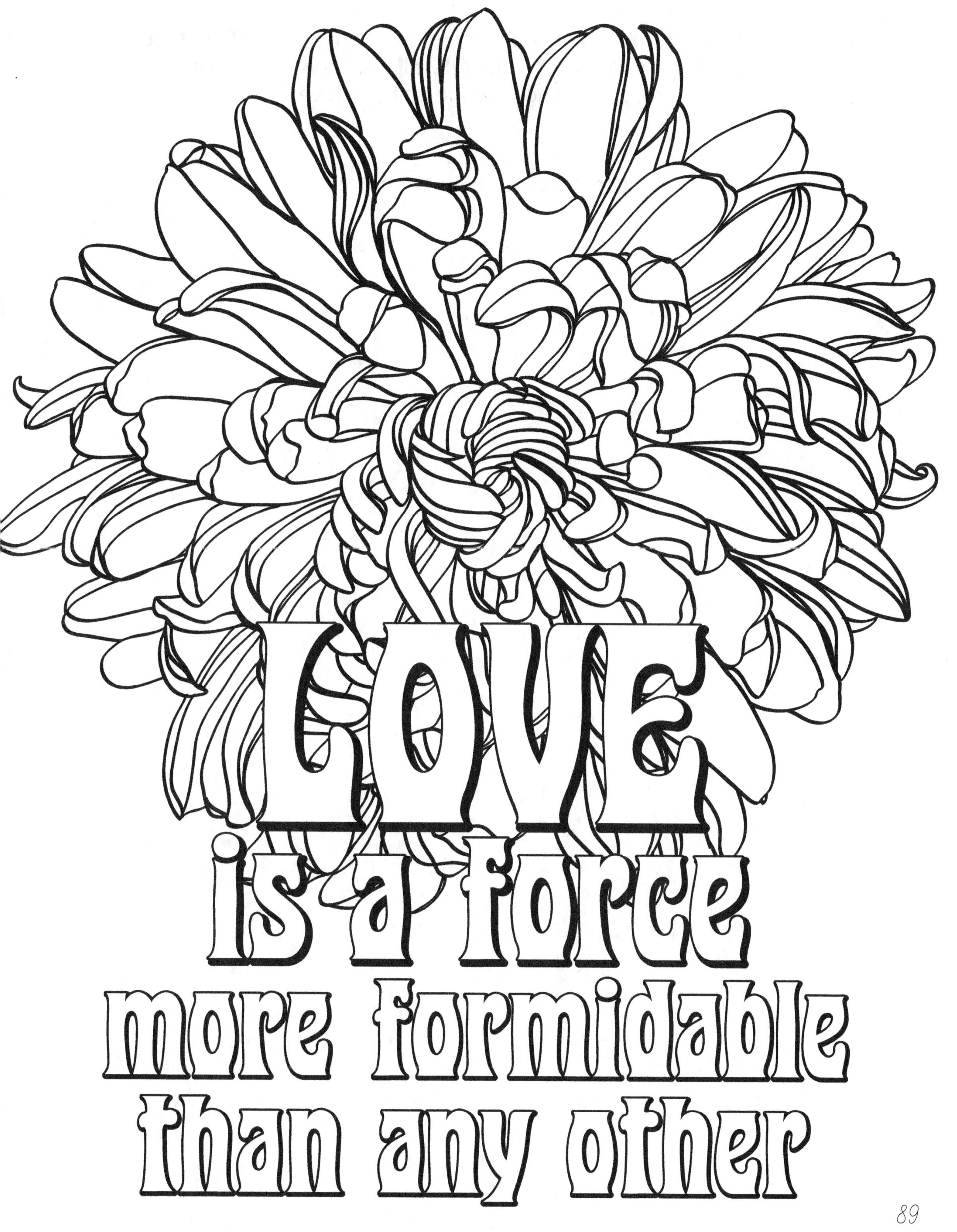
LOVE
is a force
more formidable
than any other

♥ You don't have to pretend to be someone else when you're with someone you love and someone who loves you. All walls fall down when you're together and you can do anything with the one you love.

Love is being true to ourselves

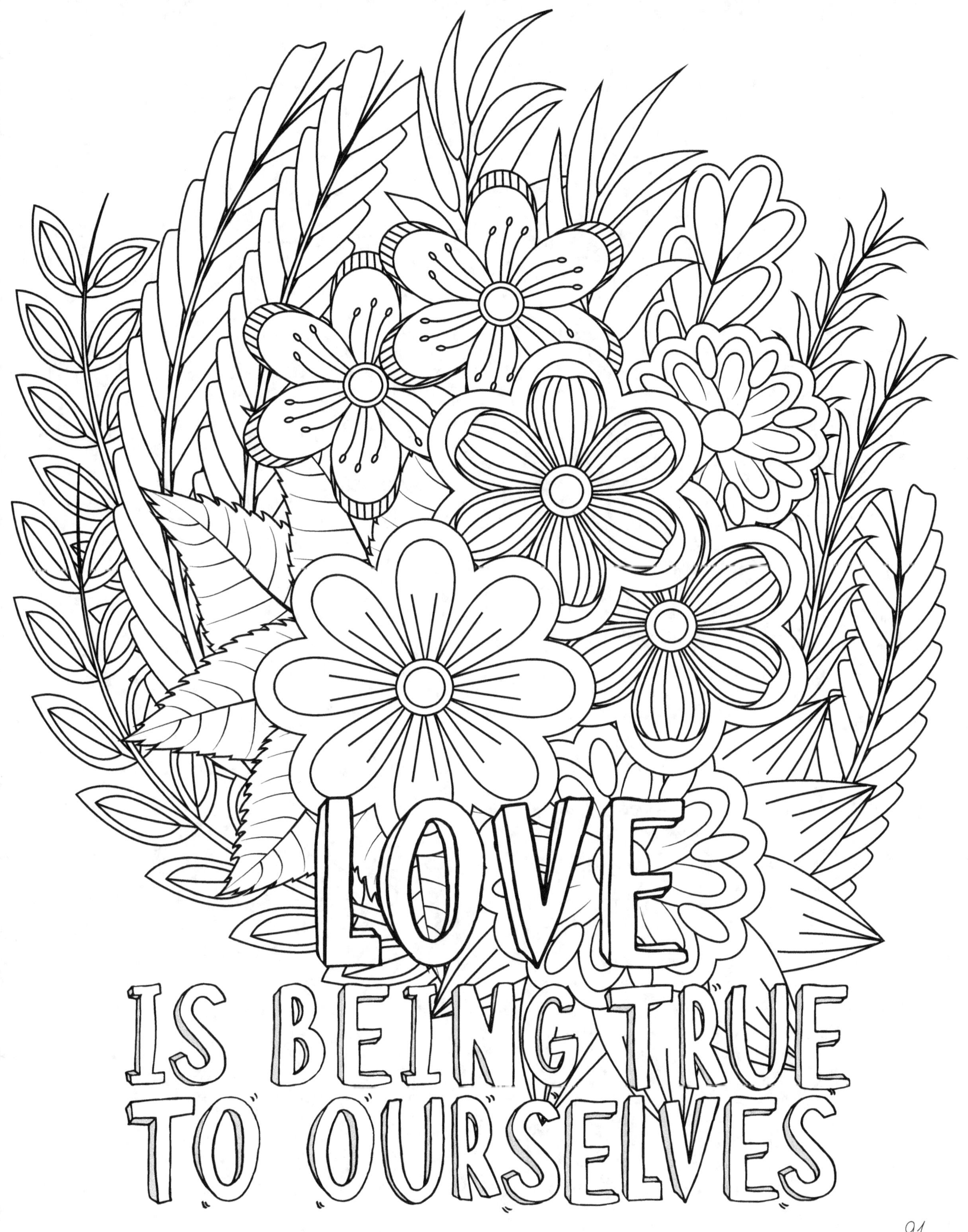

LOVE
IS BEING TRUE
TO OURSELVES

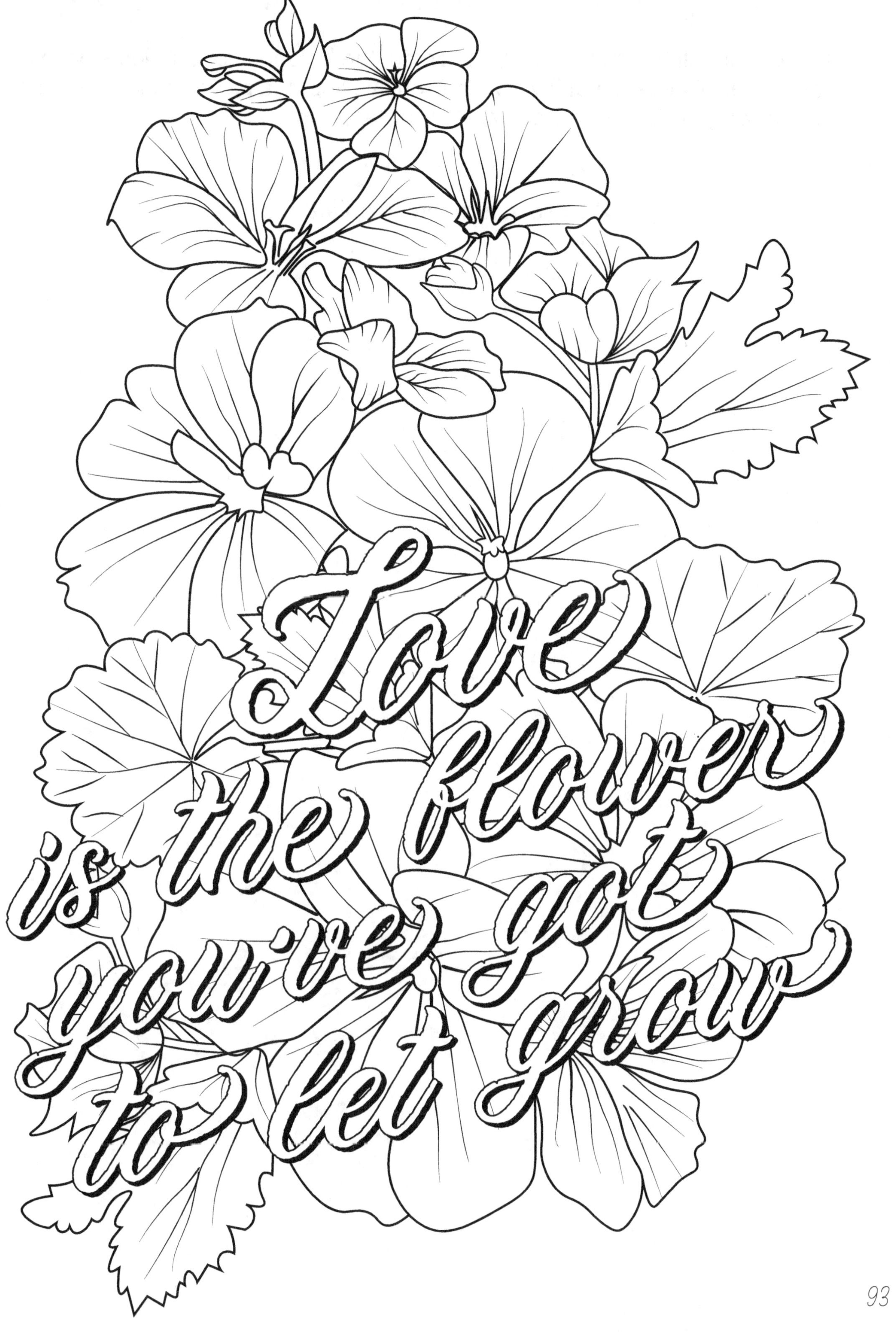

Love
is the flower
you've got
to let grow

♥ Think about all the things that you can do, the boldness of the decisions you can make, all because of love. When you live your life based on love, you can do amazing things for yourself and for other people.

Love can turn the world around

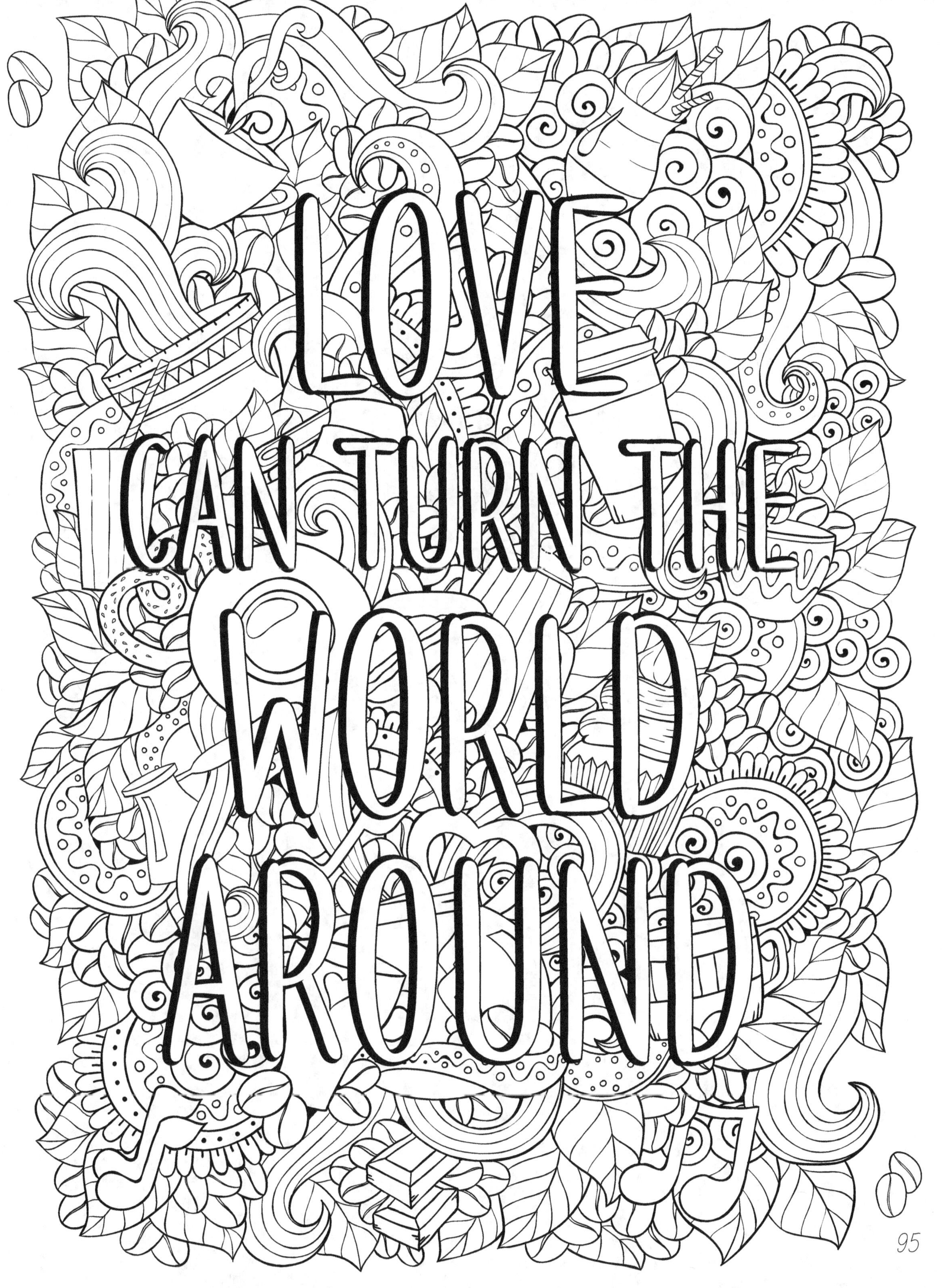

LOVE
CAN TURN THE
WORLD
AROUND

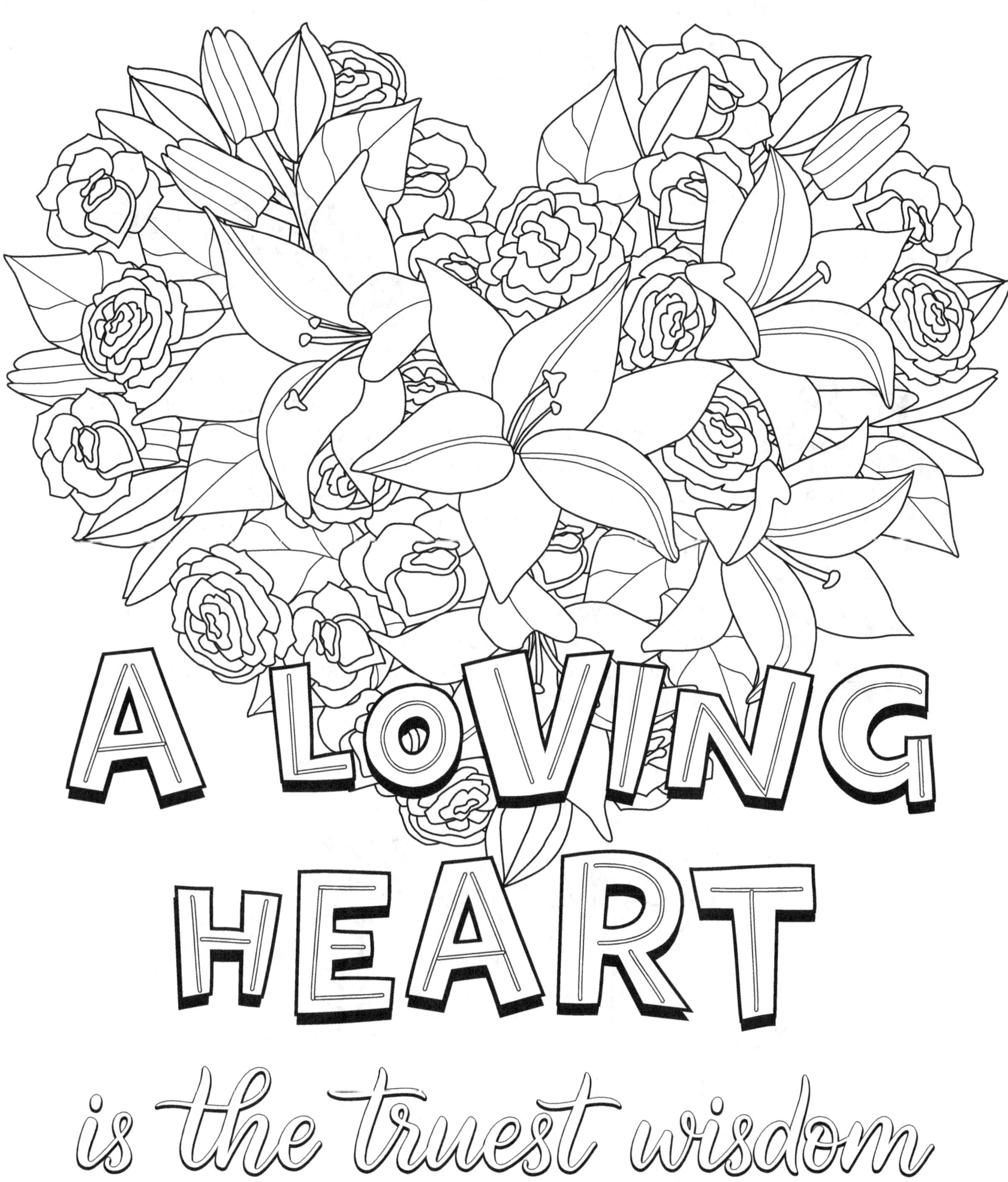
A LOVING
HEART
is the truest wisdom

CREATIVE LOVE CHALLENGES

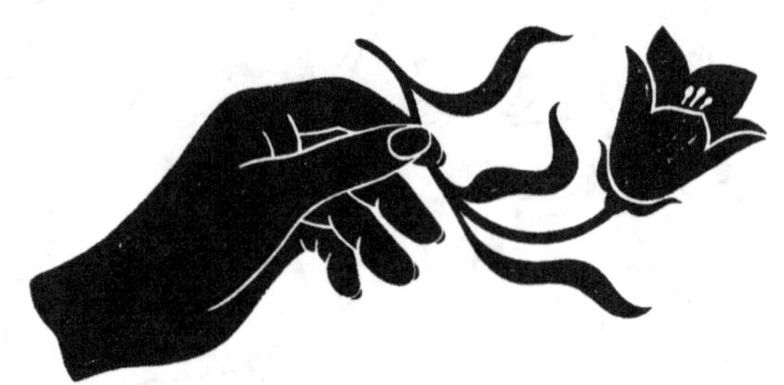

Even though this book is coming to an end,
your journey of love is just beginning!
Now is the time to experiment - create
your own compositions, make up your own
lettering, write about love, draw about love!

This chapter encourages you to step out of your stylistic comfort zone and create new alphabet decorations, new lettering styles, and new combinations of compositions that reflect how you feel about love, how you love yourself and other people, and how you experience this love. This is your safe space to practice and unleash your creativity. And when you're ready, you can share what you created!

Organize your schedules in your diary with quotes about love, give your friends cards about love.
Remember: cultivate what matters! Inspire others and spread the love!

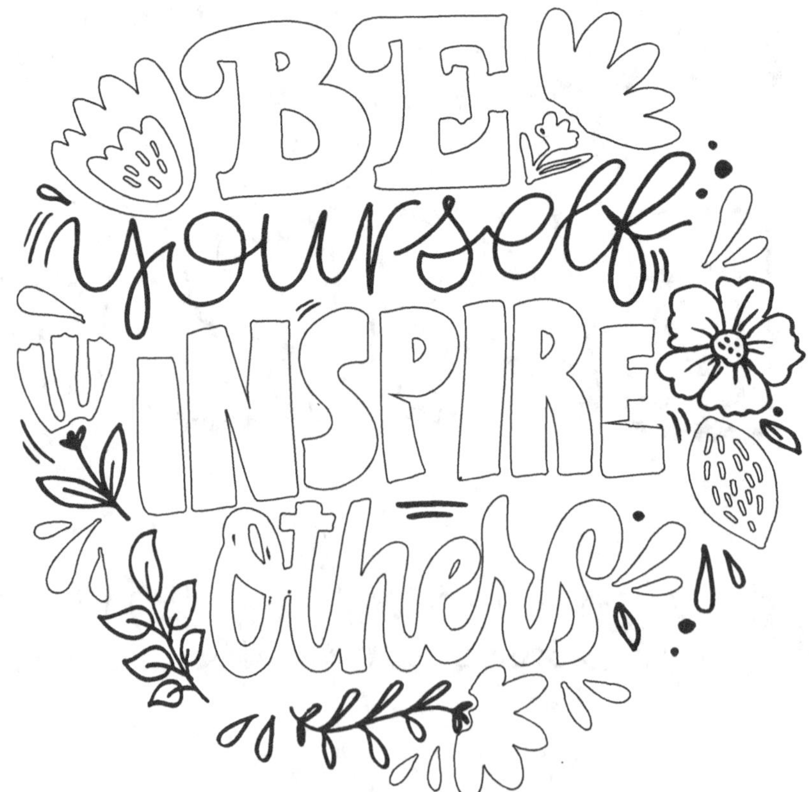

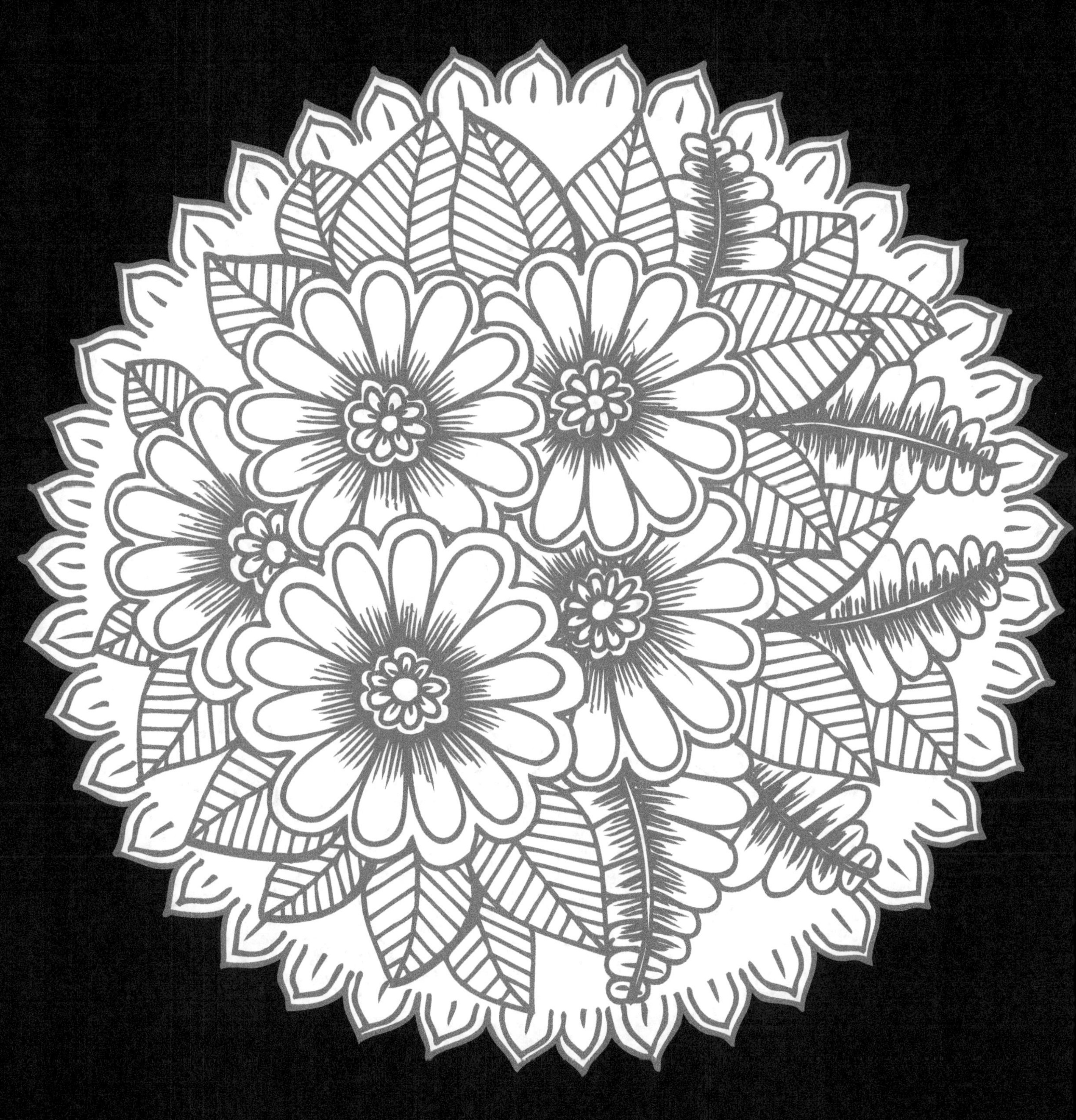

♥ Practice creating a new font by decorating the alphabet with plant elements. You are free to do it however you want.

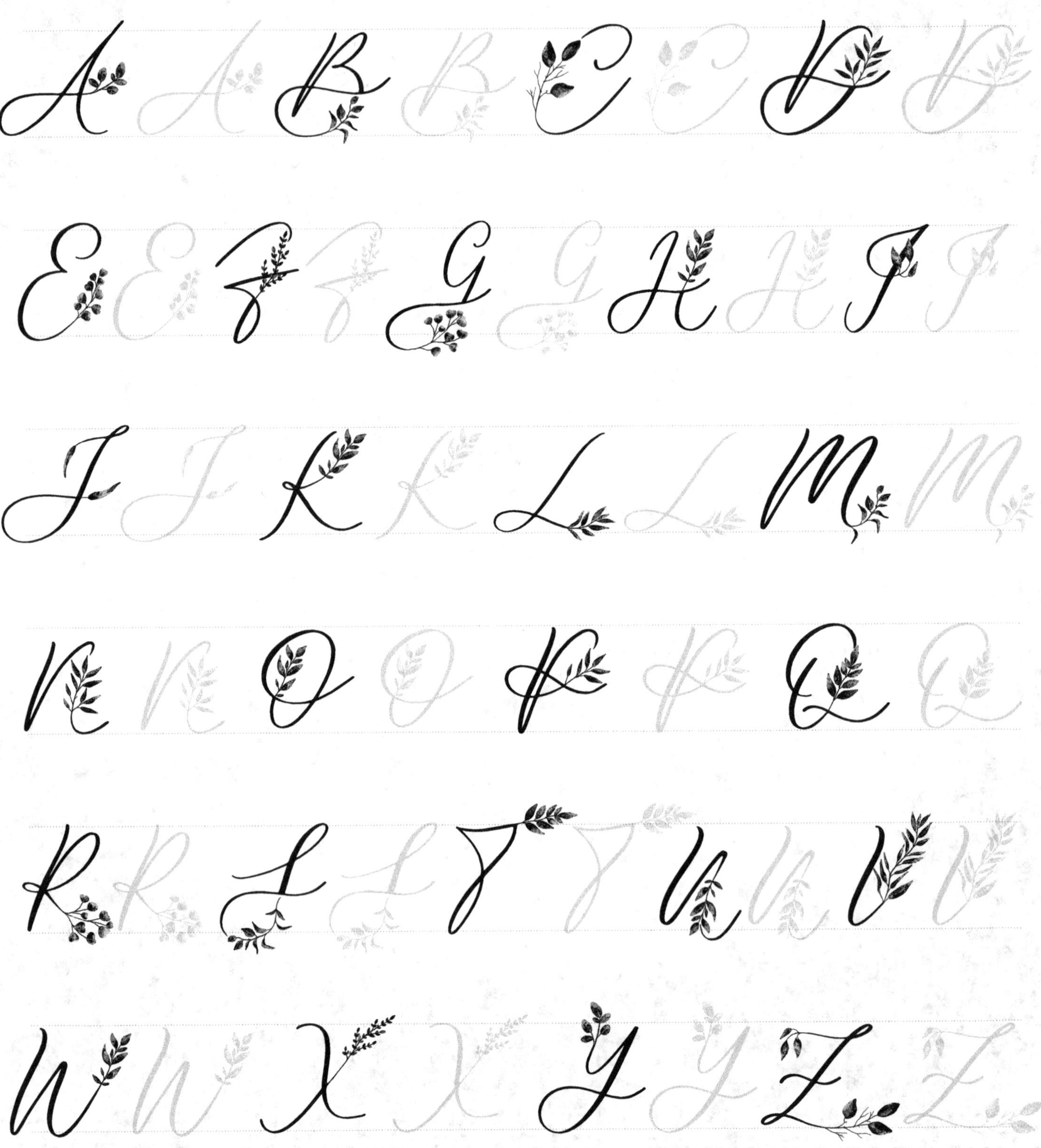

♥ Now create a font of your own. Decorate it with whatever you can associate with love.

♥ Choose a favorite affirmation or positive quote about self-love and create a lettering piece that expresses how you feel about that quote.

You have the tools and the foundations of expressing
love through calligraphy and lettering. You can now share
your work with the ones you love and those who love you.
Let your love flourish your works of art!

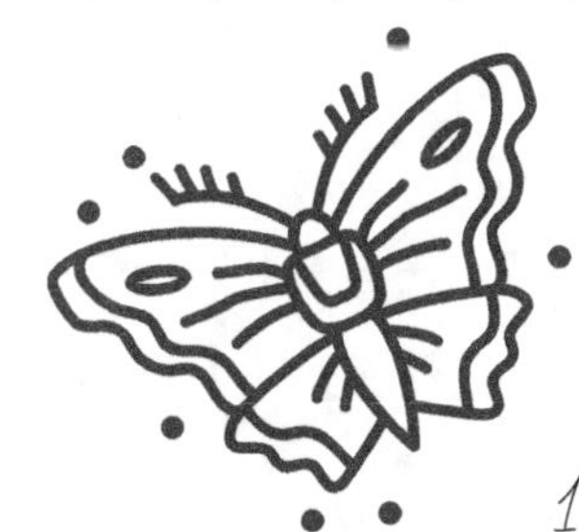

REFLECTION

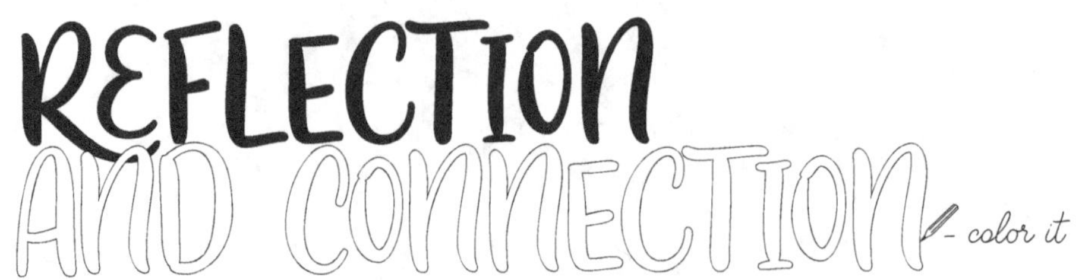

You have reached the end of Letters of Love, but it's not really the end. Through the exercises and reflections you completed, you have unlocked your power of love and self-compassion. You have honed your skills in lettering and coloring and nurtured an emotional connection with yourself. We hope your journey continues and you grow even more in embracing love and enriching your creative pursuits.

Give yourself some time to reflect on your experience with this book. Use the space provided to write down your learnings on what love and self-compassion is. How have the creative exercises helped you in learning to listen to your thoughts about love and what you believe about it? Celebrate your journey of personal growth and the connections you've made along the way.

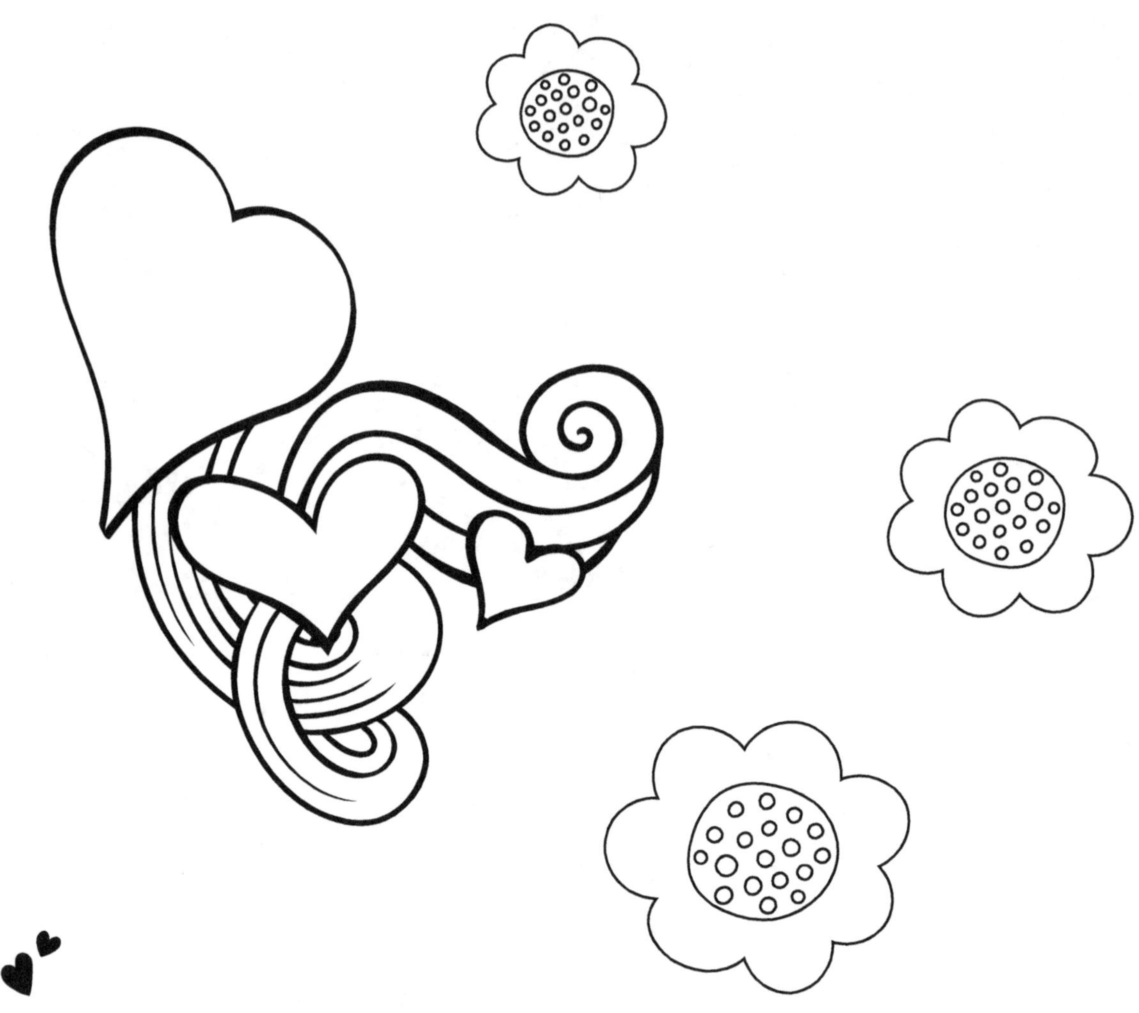

Carry the lessons of love and self-compassion with you wherever you go. Create and nurture your relationships through truthfully expressing your emotions and using your creativity to experience a full life. We look forward to walking with you through this creative journey of expression.

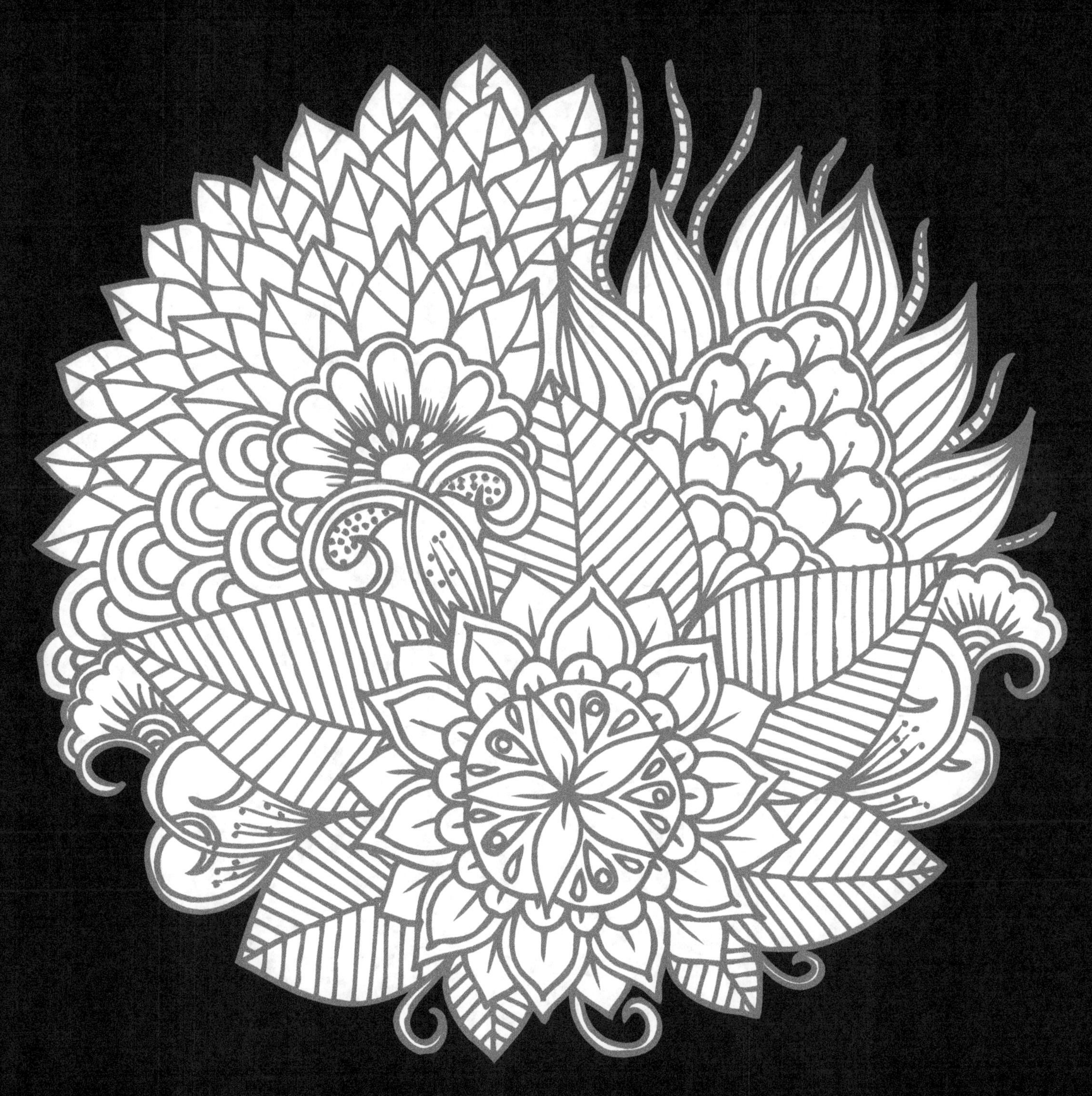

www.ingramcontent.com/pod-product-compliance
Lightning Source LLC
Chambersburg PA
CBHW060514120726
48002CB00011B/3163